BOOK OF DREAMS

Dreams, Visions and Experiences
in the Year 2020-2021

BELLA LOUISE ALLEN

authorHOUSE®

AuthorHouse™
1663 Liberty Drive
Bloomington, IN 47403
www.authorhouse.com
Phone: 833-262-8899

Published by AuthorHouse   03/16/2021

ISBN: 978-1-6655-1972-4 (sc)
ISBN: 978-1-6655-1970-0 (hc)
ISBN: 978-1-6655-1971-7 (e)

Library of Congress Control Number: 2021905150

Print information available on the last page.

This book is printed on acid-free paper.

Our Heavenly Father speaks: "In the beginning was the Word". "Jesus was there, not only before matter; he was there before time". He did not come into being; He was there before time". "He did not come into being; He just was."

"I AM; the only God, your Savior, through Jesus Christ, our Lord, be glory, majesty, dominion, and authority, before all time and now and forever."

The Creator gave us Grace in Christ, Jesus before the times of the ages.

The Lord reaches out to Bella Louise Allen in 2006. Jesus Christ comes to her to prepare her for her near-death experience six years later. Bella records the messages, visions and her experiences since that fateful day. She walked the halls of her local mental facility and finds the Lord standing, waiting for her to open her heart to Him. After her near-death experience in 2012 Jesus Christ takes over her every thought and every desire to live life. The Lord asks her one simple question and she follows His direction. Bella Louise records all that He brings to her. She conveys the messages and warnings brought forward to her since her awakening and tries to open many doors to get the messages of deep sadness to the children of the world.

Book of Dreams; will highlight the tragic events that took place in the year ending 2020-2021. The year of the horrible pandemic, history in the making. The angels surround and push her on with lessons in love from the other side. Science behind the physical body taught and understood and Bella shares some self-help techniques that helped her on her own 'spiritual emergence'. Bella was shown many things by the Lord, since 2015. The dim future was only one vision shared with her on her daily walks with Christ. Warnings and messages shared with her through her dreams by the creator and the Lord Jesus Christ. He reaches out to us all and she tries to get messages of hope, love and the promise of a better tomorrow written for the world to see. Bella Louise Allen wishes to share; *"none of us walk alone"* and *"angels do walk among us. "There is hope for a brighter tomorrow if we love one another". "Unity* *of a nation and a world will be important over the next few years, in order to bring the light back into this world".*

This book is one in a series of thirty-three books written. Highlighting the Second Coming of Jesus Christ and the worlds tragic loses in the year 2020-2021. Jesus Christ calls out to all God's children as Bella Louise Allen records His Truths and the love God has for all humanity.

Dedication

The following work is dedicated in memory of all those lives lost during the year of the Horrible Pandemic. Dedication goes out to all the grandmother's, grandfather's, mom's, dad's, aunt's, uncle's, sisters and brothers. I dedicate this book to all the children who were affected by COVID-19 in the Year 2020-2021.

This is a time in history where so many lives were lost and so much science was discovered. The year 2020-2021 will never be forgotten and the book I present to you outlines the love God; Our Father and His Son, Jesus Christ has for the children of the world. This book shines a light on God's love for all the young and old souls throughout history.

There have been many books over the years recording history by author's and scholars from all walks of life. The book I present to you here, is one of the saddest love stories written, for it walks us back through history to help us understand why we are all so loved by our Creator.

There is so much pain and sorrow today and the Lord reaches out to us from the tombs to help us all understand why He loves us so. The book I present to you is done in diary form. Love letters written from God as I cling to Him for strength. Letters written to God's children, as I come to understand my own story is very much like those who I care for daily as I work behind the scenes with the elderly. I work on the front lines taking care some of the most vulnerable of God's children. I am an in-home healthcare provider, assisting all those in need of end of life care.

These are hard times for so many, and I hold the Lord's hand. Jesus walks me back through history to help me understand our creator's great love and passion for us all. Jesus Christ helps me understand the importance for us to love and be compassionate to one another.

May we all remember why we are here. I hope to touch your lives and remind you, none of us walk alone. For the Lord endures it all with each of.

Bella Louise Allen

Review

Hopes review: On February 26, 2021, a young woman in her early twenties across the hall from my apartment studies to become a veterinarian. I ask for a review and she writes a disclaimer and states the following on my newest writings; Book of Dreams. One of thirty-three books in a series.

Disclaimer- I presently do not fall into any religion. Different perspectives from different people have always intrigued me. The story of Robin (Lily) within this story, was very powerful. It was an eye- opening experience for me. I got chills when you were explaining how things connected together. The world works in mysterious ways. I have always been a believer of Karma. What you put into the world matters. I believe what goes around comes around. I also believe the energy and vibes that you send into the world do effect people.

One thing that I think may be helpful as well as interesting is if you include information on what stones/crystals you are using for Reiki in the section you talk about what you were using for Betty's healing session. Like what they mean and what they do for your chakras. As somebody who has no knowledge of how Reiki works, this would be helpful to better understand.

Hope asks: Have you listened to Lewis Capaldi?

He is also a blue-eyed soul singer like Adele. I wrote a research paper on him in the fall and he writes beautiful songs.

Your writings are so passionate and engaging. Even to a non-religious reader, it was an eye- opening read for me!

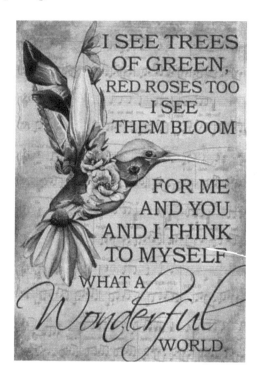

The Year of the Horrible Pandemic of 2020-2021

Quote: *No single battle ever took so many lives of God's children. No one event every brought so many children back to His cross. The unity of the world was felt by Our Creator even if it was not always portrayed as the truth…*
Bella Louis Allen

Quote: *Light and shadow are opposite sides of the same coin. We can illuminate our paths or darken our way. It is our choice.*
Maya Angelou-*One of the greatest women in history*

Acknowledgement

I want to honor my own mother. I want to honor my grandmother's, Aunts, and my daughter. I want to honor my granddaughter's, and my sisters. I want to acknowledge all the women God has placed in my life along the way. It is our stories and great love that helps form the strong bond of family over the many generations. I want to highlight all the women who touched my life over the years. Women who helped form and mold my own beliefs of *'love conquers all'*. No matter how many times life can knock you down. We women continue to rise above all life's challenges.

Nurses, doctors, housewives, childcare providers, CEO"s, Vice President's, teachers, healthcare workers, and grocery clerks. Too many professions to mention and so much wisdom shared over the years. It is these stories that have touched my life that I would like to highlight. Strong bold women making a difference in the lives of everyone we touch; on a daily basis.

A message to all women: Keep on shining your light and spread it for we certainly need your love and light in this world as we continue to figure out how to come out of all the darkness portrayed over the past two years.

Bella Louise Allen- I am a spiritual child of God. I am a mother, grandmother, aunt, daughter and a sister...

Contents

Preface

A heartwarming inspiring book erupts from my heart today. February 14, 2021. I come to realize my true gifts lie in speaking, communicating and writing for the Lord. Our Creator and the Great I AM.

Coming through my own 'spiritual emergence', which started back in the year 2006, and today I realize I am right where God needs me to be.

Today is the day celebrated around the world for lovers, husbands, and wives. Even the little children celebrate Valentine's Day! Our children have tiny hearts with a great big purpose. I have come to learn over the years of God's deep love for each of His children. I learn over the course of my life we are all created to love and be light, for we come from The Light!

I open another chapter in my life this morning. I have worked tirelessly for the past fifteen years to find myself. I heard the Lord knocking on my door and it became very loud in the year 2006. I had busied myself beyond belief and I was lost in this world struggling to survive and make ends meet. I was in the midst of raising three beautiful children and trying desperately to hold together a failing marriage.

The further I ran and the harder I worked the louder the Lord knocked on my door. I could feel things, I knew things, and I experienced what is called the 'Great Awakening'. As I ran faster and faster my inner world and reality began to switch into overdrive. I began to feel my inner world and the outer world crash in around me. The Spiritual Emergency began.

My calling from God was becoming evident. In 2006, my need to help, succeed and overcome all obstacles in my life ended up bringing me to my knees. I experienced for the next eleven years the 'spiritual warfare' that I had heard of. The 'Spiritual Emergency' kicked in full gear and fast forward. I ended up at our local mental facility three times. Over the course of the next eight years I would go in and come out of the hospital. I had my first vision of Jesus Christ while in the hospital. I was drawn up out of bed by a young man calling out for help on the unit. I walked down the hallway in search of this man calling out. On my way to this man I saw Jesus Christ. His beautiful figure was standing in front of me. I knelt and kissed His feet and I went right back to bed like it was nothing. That one vision was preparing me for my near-death experience that occurred six years later, in March of 2012.

I have found out the difference between a near death experience and a true death experience. I found my 'true death experience' was a shift that I found to be happening within me by my creator. My spirit had died. In March of 2012 after gastric bypass surgery. I had three surgeries in four weeks and my soul transitioned on the table during the second surgery. My spirit that was trying to fight to stay in this world, exited my body. When I crossed over to the other side, I found I did not come back alone. The transition of my soul took place that day. I became enlightened to who I was, where I came from and then I was shown by Jesus Christ why I was created.

Since 2015 I have written about my life experiences. I have learned what automatic writing is. I have learned I do not walk alone. I have learned the 'angels' make up who I AM. I learned since my NDE; I have come to completely understand my true death experience. I understand that I have gifts and talents lying underneath all this 'physical body'. I have struggled to love and care for 'me', since my birth in July of 1967.

On this journey into the Light of I Am, I found I am a scientist, a doctor, a healer, a counselor, a nurse, a musician, a theologian, a budding painter and artist, and I am a prolific writer. The greatest thing I am, is a child of God, a mother and grandmother. I found on my journey all the experiences in my life was to prepare me for the truths I found out the day I stood in the Light of my Creator!! The day I stood in THE LIGHT of I AM…

This book will shine a light on the aspects of who I am. How it is put together and the passages written within in it I will leave up to the GREATER I AM. I will leave it in God; the Father's hands. Today on the 14th day of February in the year 2021; I write about the LOVE that I came to BE!!

CHAPTER 1

Mentoring Through Social Media

Sharing Knowledge as the Lord

directs my answers...

I have been counseling and giving advice to those in search of hope most of my life. A gift the Lord has been assisting me with since He created me. Today I start a book of the proof of His love for each of us. I write and counsel others as the Lord, Our God directs me.

Working in the healthcare field for thirty-four years prepared me to open my heart fully to all those the Lord placed in front of me. Taking care of the elderly was where I first started. In high school I attended the nursing program and received my Certified Nursing Assistant Certificate. A job that would change my life and connect me to many stories just like my own.

I lost my grandmother at an early age and it broke my heart. A generation of God's children nearly gone now. My grandparents were from the late 1890's and early 1900's. Grammie Stone was born in August of 1902. My grandfather I never met. He was a hard- working Mainer and he owned his own sawmill in a small unorganized territory in the backwoods of Maine. There was never a local store in the town I grew up in. There was only a one room red barn that schooled the towns children. Mom called it 'the little red schoolhouse'. Growing up I would walk by this little old red schoolhouse. A building abandoned and I'm sure there were many memories within the four walls of that school. I could see the red paint was fading away each year as I walked back and forth over the years.

My connection to the elderly and the dying is what set me up for the next steps in my life. A career I never would have dreamed of before my true death experience. I am now a certified Reiki Master Practitioner and an in-home healthcare provider for the elderly. In addition to taking care of the elderly; I currently work with women in need of spiritual mentoring and centering in the Light of their creator. I provide a safe place for them to come and work through their pain and trauma.

Death can take a toll on the very spirit of each of us. I have come to understand this through my own experiences with death and losing so many at such a young age. Taking care of the elderly, I could never put a number to how many special souls I have assisted in the transition from this world into the next. I just know It has been amazing and enlightening as I went from fearing death to accepting it as a natural part of the cycle of life. Then I finally came to understand death can be a release from this painful world we seem to live in.

Touching people's hearts is what I love to do. I love to bring them knowledge of how I overcame childhood abuse. I love to share my story of success. I like to share how I became my own hero in a world that tried to drown out my voice and nearly killed my own spirit and tender soul.

In this book I will share inspiring stories of those I have encountered over the years. I will share questions and answers of life, death and how to deal with the pain of it all. I will share with you some healing techniques that have helped me and some of my clients. I aid others in self-help techniques. I help them understand that we do have the power within ourselves to overcome all the darkness that tries so desperately to keep us prisoner in this world.

I will share with you messages from special angels as the Lord leads me on my daily walks. I record messages from the angels and the experiences I encounter as I help others try to understand the darkness and negativity in their own lives. Special souls the Lord places in my own circle. People in search of love, light and the Lord.

May you find these stories uplifting and encouraging and may you learn a few things about why you were sent to incarnate in this world. May you understand you never walk alone and if you open your heart and mind, you can see a wonderful world unfold before your own eyes.

Remember your loved ones are *only a whisper away*. Please know we never walk alone, and the angels wait in the wings and sit on the clouds waiting for us to call them in.

Mentoring Through Social Media

Proof of Life After Death

B.D. asks:

I'm so scared of death. Life is losing its light, there is so much darkness now.

I respond: To B.D. who is struggling to find the light in this world. Her world is being consumed by the darkness and I try to give her encouragement today.

RE: My responds to questions.

Re: other's respond and give input.

RE: The darkness is in this world, not the next. We humans forget to create the light, hold the light and be the light. So, we see the darkness. We must remember where we came from. We must hold the light within us. Don't magnify what we see or feel in this world. Focus, fill and surround yourself with the beauty and light that is still here. That's how we create more light in this darker world we seem to be living in.

B.D.:

I used to feel the beauty but people changed. What I see is the darkness in the world. It is self-centered, fake, and uncaring. This world, no one cares about the poor and homeless and suffering. It's all a bunch of fake people.

RE: I feel your pain and knowing. I have experienced that part of this world. I see it and feel it. I get up every day to help others. I hope every day to make a difference in someone's life. Not all are awake to what they are here for. I hope God will bring you all you need today.

B.D.:

re- I pray every day to see this in people. I'm still waiting.

RE: It will come. God promises. He is lifting the darkness right now!!

Proof of Life After Death

L.N.B. asks:

What does it mean when you may be facing death, but you're clinging to life?

RE: Depending on what stage of death you're in physically. I have seen souls stuck in the vortex. These souls are scared to die. Their souls fear the transition and the soul twirls and fights letting go of the last strand attached to their physical body. I walked into a room of dying patient and as I came up to the side of her bed, the energy field around her was holding her in this world. She was an atheist who did not have knowledge of who she was or why she was here. She had no '*faith or belief system*' of what or who she was.

Her soul was literally fighting to let go of her body. I felt this woman's soul not wanting to let go of her physical body. That's why it's important to not fear death. The lighter the soul is the easier the transition will be. It's just a transition from this physical world (which can be very painful). We come from the LIGHT. The Mothership so to speak.

YOUR SOUL GUIDES YOU

S. S. asks:

YOUR THOUGHTS ON ANGER?

Last night on 'Soul Talk' we spoke on what is unfolding during COVID-19, including anger. Anger is the power behind our empowerment. I know for me, I have not always honored anger, nor allowed it to surface. Not that I do not get angry, but I suppress it, divert it. I feel anger is an emotion to be controlled and not always worthy to express.

Denying myself my own anger suppressed a real part of me. It did not make the anger go away, but rather go, 'underground', resurfacing in other ways, not always healthy or helpful ways.

Thinking about anger after last night's discussion; I realized I was denying a part of me. It is as if I was not worthy to have anger. It was as if I was confronting a learned behavior from childhood.

And two, by allowing anger to be one of a myriad of acceptable emotions, it opened the gates for anger to be expressed in a healthy, constructive way, while also consciously giving permission for other's to have anger too. A beautiful revelation and one that will help me to continue to clear my own "filter" of what blocks my soul patterns.

Thoughts on Anger?

I respond:

RE: I have been allowed to understand my emotions from all angles. Fear, anxiety, hunger, thirst, failure, anger, and grief. I breath in. I breath it out. I feel that emotion. The emotion coming in. I ask, "what is it"? I ask, "where is it coming from"? I ask, "what lesson am I feeling coming from this emotion"? I look at it and learn from it. I release it by breathing through it. I visually see it (the emotion and where it has come from; childhood, marriage, kids, a situation that I feel is out of control, and I let it go, visually). If this lesson or emotion comes back, I do a self-check. Gut first, heart and then I see if I can release it sooner than last time. I ask myself, "How am I feeling about that 'emotion', 'situation' or 'experience'? I do a self-check of how differently I am 'reacting' to that emotion. I release and surrender it up for it still is only an emotion. 'This too shall pass'. We have the power to grow from that experience if we look at it from the angle of 'what is the lesson'. What is it teaching me about me? Our reaction is what makes the emotion hold us or release us so we can grow on our journey. We can do better with our anger if we look at it from where it is coming from and then we will be better equipped next time that feeling, memory or emotion pops up.

YOUR SOUL GUIDES YOU- Administration responds to my RE:- Yes!!! It is always an opportunity and it will always pass. Thank you for your wonderful and very wise observations. Love to you.

RE: Love to you as well. It is time to pass on Christ's Knowledge of love conquers fear. If we allow love in…

J.G.

Re: That is so powerful and true!!

PROOF OF LIFE AFTER DEATH

H. H. asks:

I just took a picture in my daughter's room. She just passed away recently. There is nothing red in that room what did this mean?

The photo shows a large red circular light on the wall. The photo is dark. The lighting in the room is dark. On the wall in the photo is the appearance of the *"Red Light Rays"*.

RE: This is an angel's presence. The color red in the rays' spectrum is an Archangel's aura. There is the presence of the Being, *"Archangel Uriel"*. Uriel is being presented to you. The angel of Wisdom. Who is very present in my own circle of Archangel's. He/she is presenting themselves, so you are aware of your daughter's presence. Which is a lower vibrational being now. The Higher Vibrational Beings will bring the lower vibrational beings to us. To communicate.

C. C. asks:

Re: How does one research the archangels?

RE: Google Archangel Uriel. Research this angel. He/she wants to communicate with you. The Angel of Wisdom, the Red Ray of Light…

PROOF OF LIFE AFTER DEATH

D. G. asks:

I've always been curious, do we go straight to another life after death?

RE: After our transition there is a holding space after our review. The Creator goes over our life with us. There is an adjustment period for our soul. Time does not exist beyond this world. The soul then, after the 3-days, 'earth time', which no one knows of this *'reel'* time, for time is an illusion. We are shown our next life and we have the opportunity to accept or deny the incarnation. We are then guided to the next incarnation by the *'Light'*...

Whether in this world, or another.

PROOF OF LIFE AFTER DEATH

N. M. asks:

When they say family comes to meet you when you pass, what about the family that you cut out of your life when you were living? Do they come to you too? I really hope not.

RE: Before we can enter the Light from which we came, the review will prepare you for your next step. Your ego and fear will no longer be a part of you. All that pained you. All that broke you will be gone. You will be Light. So, yes you will be reunited with those of your family which you cut out of your life, or those that cut you out. For we are love. We come from LOVE and we will return to LOVE...

PROOF OF LIFE AFTER DEATH

M. D. asks:

Since my dad died in April 2020, my siblings and I have had a falling out and are no longer speaking. I feel they did me wrong while my dad was sick and blame me for a lot of things. I had no control over. I want to let it go but can't. I need my dad to show me somehow or give me some sign that he doesn't blame me, and that he was proud of me in the end with how I handled things. I can't have peace with his death until I know he doesn't feel the way they do. Or if he did, I need to know that too. Does anyone know of any particular sign that a spirit would use to show this?

RE: Father spirit comes forward in my world as the black and white dragonfly. He flies and flutters around you daily. His heart is part of your heart. Please forgive them. Please forgive me. Please forgive yourself. No one is to blame. My choices. You absolutely did your best through it all. Fear and broken hearts led to their actions. Please call me. Dad is only a whisper away. Sit with me. Let me hug you. Let my wings wrap around you. Let that fear and pain go, it hurts my heart when it hurts your heart. (I feel a burning sensation in my stomach).

PROOF OF LIFE AFTER DEATH

S. N. asks:

So how many people believe in reincarnation? If so, what made you decide this?

RE: Yes, I do. Jesus Christ taught me that reincarnation is true.

S.N.

re: Please explain?

RE: I have been walking in between the world's ever since my true death experience. In March of 2012 I had gastric bypass surgery. I had two additional surgeries to save my life, (body). After my release from the hospital it took me three months to recover from this surgery that was supposed to be a three to five-day light duty work, surgery recover time. I had three surgeries in four weeks. It took three months to recover after my last surgery and many weeks in the hospital.

Jesus Christ has been calling me all my life. I knew it. Everyone in my life kept shutting that door. Because they had the wrong knowledge of who He is. I have been learning many truths from Him since 2006, when I had my first vision of Him. I started what they call the spiritual emergence. The chaos in my life brought me to my knees. Three times I fell with my cross. Just like the Lord did. I had three hospitalizations for 'imbalance'. I was put on medication to bring me back to reality of this painful world. Which I was trying to escape. Once that hard journey in waking up, and after my hospitalizations and then having my true death experience, Jesus Christ came to life within me. His voice became louder than the radio I would listen to. His voice came to me and through me and He started teaching me science of the body.

"TRIAD OF DEATH", is the word He gave me to explain my death experience. That's what happened to my physical body in March of 2012.

After much soul searching and many nights of vivid dreams and constant communication the Lord proved to me my soul has been here since before the beginning of time, as we as human beings know it.

I have written thirty-three books since 2015. When Jesus asked me to record our communication and His lessons.

Jesus showed me certain lives I have lived. He showed me I had written books for our Creator/Heavenly Father before. I was having bleed through of memories before my true death experience. I was having communication with different aspects of my other souls. It was a very intense spiritual emergence. That turned into an emergency three times. I knew what was happening. No one in the medical field explained it to me. Jesus Christ, my Lord; God and Savior taught me that re-incarnation is The Holy Spirit… through me… with me… and in me…

I hope that helped.

That is only a glimpse of what He has taught me. He is the Most-High. He is the Almighty Everlasting Light of this world and beyond…

O. C. asks:

re: Well it was part of Christianity teachings for several hundred years until it became inconvenient for the power structure.

RE: It's certainly been interesting. My first counseling session with my priest, Jesus Christ and I asked about re-incarnation and incarnate, which was four years ago. Subjects over my head, so I thought. Memories of who I AM came flooding in and the Catholic Church has all thirty-three books of my communication with Jesus Christ. I am waiting on a call for my first three books to be adapted into a movie. Christ promises me movies, documentaries and best seller books. I hold Him tight to that promise. He shows me it's coming to live stream soon!!

re: An icon with its mouth wide open...

RE: That's what Jesus is hoping for. Surprise. Not too many people today understand the 'Real Jesus Christ', within us all quite the way I do.

re: I can't wait to read your books!!

PROOF OF LIFE AFTER DEATH

C. B. asks:

I met with a medium a few months ago. It was a great experience. She was soooo spot on. I wanted to schedule another family session for my sisters to join but they all say some evil spirits come through imitating loved ones. Is this true?

RE: I have been a sceptic in the past as well. It wasn't until I had my own experience and started having visions and the knowing that has helped me to understand how a medium becomes gifted. After my own spiritual emergence and my awakening, I struggled for eleven years to understand all that was coming in through the veil. Once I learned to center in Jesus Christ and to bring in the high-ranking angels (Archangels) it was difficult to know who was good or of the light. What was of a higher vibration and if someone was showing up that was 'evil' or not.

There are some mediums that are more knowledgeable of what their gifts are. There are some that have been doing this for a long time. I would just make sure your medium or seer is of good reputation and then let your own gut guide you for we all come with guiding, guardian angels and higher ranking (archangel's) and angels.

THE HIGHLY PERCEPTIVE COLLECTIVE

S. C. asks:

What keeps you balanced?

RE: Jesus Christ holds me in center.

Others respond:

1. Myself

2. Yoga, meditation, and journaling

3. Meditation

4. Movement and playing with children

5. Spending time in nature.

6. Being at the beach or the mountains, or in nature.

7. Believing in a magical world. The power in our hearts and the magic in our souls.

8. Walking, dancing, daily breath work and toning.

PROOF OF LIFE AFTER DEATH

T.M. K. asks:

Sometimes I often wonder if maybe there is nothing after we die. Maybe the 'signs' we see/hear are just our minds telling us that we are seeing/hearing signs just to help us cope with our pain. Does anyone ever think this?

RE: I work with the elderly that cross over from this reality to the Light of Truth. Is see, feel and experience things that are amazing. This world is a multi-dimensional reality. I had a near death experience which I call my true death and awakening of the light within me. Many truths were illuminated for me since then. My reality is the dimensions.

Walking into the past while I live in the present. It prepares me for the future.

re: I've talked and seen spirits. The dead come to me also, as I dream they give me warnings or tell me someone, a grandmother or friend wants to talk to them.

PROOF OF LIFE AFTER DEATH

A.M. asks:

I'm getting more and more down with my worry and anxiety about, life and death. I beg my loved ones who have passed to come to me. Nothing happens. I need more than a bird or a butterfly. I wish so badly I could see them, at least once.

RE: Loved ones usually show up in our dreamtime. They will show up when we step out of our ego or fear. Recognize and record some of your dreams. It will help invite them in also ask if your guardian angel Saint Michael or your guiding angels will assist you. They love for us to ask for their assistance with this process.

Meditation is what wakes your senses to the spirit world. It can invite those beings into your world. Ask for protection from the lower realms. Always surround and protect yourself with your Christ Conscious, Jesus Christ wants you to be at peace with your loved ones who have crossed. It is so different and not nearly as bad as some are misled to believe.

Open your mind to the Light and the Light will be shown to you.

re: Sometimes we try too hard. I know I do at times and everything stops. When I relax and just believe then they come again.

RE: We all wish the same. If only I could see them. How much easier our lives would be. All we can do is believe what the NDE's are telling us repeatedly. There is an afterlife our loved ones are there waiting for us. May God bless you. <3

PROOF OF LIFE AFTER DEATH

R. D. asks:

I wonder why so many people get a chance to see Jesus or the afterlife? I want a turn. I may not come back if given the option. Most stories all sound the same. Also sounds like people waiting for judgement possibly if people are waiting in line I will be there some day, but I love hearing everyone's experiences.

RE: Christy, you have the opportunity to see Him and experience Him. That's where prayer and meditation come in. The power to believe is how it happens. 'Ask and your will receive'. Sit and quiet your mind. Hold His picture. Look deep into His eyes. Connect your heart to your Co- Creators heart and He will show Himself to you. You need to open your heart to Him fully and He will illuminate your world with His Light. My first vision of Jesus was before my NDE, I believe He was preparing me for our meeting in the afterlife.

PROOF OF LIFE AFTER DEATH

B. J. asks:

Hey all, forgive me if I already asked this in this group. I'm trying to find out if we choose our death before coming into an earth life. I'm asking for a friend whose daughter died in a car crash. Thank you.

RE: Our path is already planned. We are sent to experience life on earth. Predestined and preplanned. You have a purpose and it's your soul path to connect to your higher consciousness to help you remember why you came. We came to love and enlighten this world with our love.

PROOF OF LIFE AFTER DEATH

M. M. Asks:

Not long after my sister died I was in bed asleep and woke up to see what seemed to be an angel with long blonde hair and wings. She smiled at me and nodded her head and then she disappeared and was gone. She was so beautiful, is this possible in our realm to see an angel?

RE: Angles surround us all. They will present themselves in many ways. We open our hearts and mind and they truly walk among us. I feel, see, hear and know of them. They are only a whisper away. Call them to you and open your heart and listen and observe. They want us to communicate with them.

PROOF OF LIFE AFTER DEATH

C. D. asks:

I'd like some insights here. Several months ago, I woke up in the middle of the night to see a hooded figure standing at the foot of my bed. The left arm was out. I started screaming and it disappeared. I googled 'hooded entities' and discover this to be a fairly common apparition-recorded for centuries. So common that there's even a children's book about them. They are called Shadow Men.

Several weeks ago, it appeared next to my bed. I could have touched it. Again, I screamed, and it disappeared.

The explanation's range from time traveler, inter-dimensional beings, demons, etc. Can anyone share their experience or knowledge about this?

RE: Archangel Azrael has appeared to me as the 'Grim Reaper'. I have seen the dark and the light of that which is beyond the veil. For me he was teaching me it does exist. The entities and spirit of darkness. I just try to listen and learn. I ask those who show up, what do you want me to know. I feel I am well protected by Christ Light for He comes first in my life. It's been a hard journey for me until I let Him Light my world up with His love. I hope that helps.

K. L. asks:

re: I am currently in the middle of writing my third novel. It's called Dark Man. My family and I have seen him several times. He usually comes when people are at their weakest. I've been researching him and he's not a good entity. He's there to try to break you down spiritually and snatch your soul.

CRYSTAL HEALING KNOW YOUR STONES.COM

Omg. Yesterday I removed a deity picture from my bedroom thinking that he is not helping me in my life. I put a black tourmaline under my pillow and slept. I had a horrible long dream of suffering in captivity with evil ghosts and some people I know were getting their blood sucked and they turned us into white ghosts.

What do you make of this?

RE: Only Jesus can save us from the darkness. Been there done it. It's not fun. Sorry for your scary dreams.

re: Drop the 'only'.

B. B. responds: Really?

RE: Yes, I was experiencing the dark night of the soul for eleven years. My first vision of Christ was preparing me for my NDE six years later. I took three months to recover from that experience and have learned many things about myself and the reason I have been incarnated this lifetime. My dreams outlined this lifetime and where I'm going. Important lessons brought forward through our dreams. Our consciousness connects directly to source energy and it wants us to know our own truths....

re: Yeaaaaaah, can we not force our religions on other people?

M.A M. re: I really don't think coming here is the best place for you to be spouting god is the only god cuz u will get lots of hell for it... I'm trying to be nice about it.

RE: Not religion. I'm a child of God. Source Light first.

re: Please! Religious discrimination/preaching/etc. We have freedom of religion in the U.S., so honor that. Blessed B.

A. C. responds:

re: The dreams reflect metaphors of energies within you. Maybe learn the lesson of the dreams and things will get better.

RE: Yesssss!!!

re: Wow! I really needed this, thanks.

E. G: asks:

So, what happens if you don't believe in Jesus?

RE: We all need things to help us along on this journey. It can be very overwhelming. I use Jesus to lean on when nothing else works. The power in belief is something He taught me. The properties in mother earths rocks He taught me do help and aid and assist in healing the body.

Yet, again it takes more than a pill or a rock or even encouragement. It takes power of your thoughts and belief's. If we use all these tools together we become powerful healers. I use stones and crystals in my Reiki Practice, healing of the hands, something Jesus and the angels led me too after my three hospitalizations. Imbalance of the brain, fear and chaos took over my life. I was kept in fear by my doctor's. Jesus led me out of fear and taught me I am my greatest healer. Rocks and crystals and essential oils are all important natural remedies to a healthier body. Believing in yourself is your greatest power. Jesus is my go-to-tool. Nothing I try to push on anyone. I'm sorry I offended anyone. That is never my intention. Jesus is my 'rock'.

C.A.L. responds:

re: Well said and I completely agree.

D.V.M. responds:

re: Same here! You have no idea how much backlash I get from my Christian acquaintances. Telling me it's the work of you know who. Jesus showed me the way to Kundalini Reiki, Crystals and sound frequencies as well as meditation. Things He learned from Yogis, monks and teachers as he grew in his lifetime.

They are missing out on so many things.

RE: Oh, boy! My heart hurt to feel His Knowledge of this. I was just writing about the experience as you chimed in. He watches everything I do and teaches me copious amounts of information. I work with many deities. He just happens to be my center and my leader in knowledge. We are all enlightened in different ways. I try to follow the law of love every day. Thank you for sharing. That's what we came for. To love. To share and to remember.

CHAPTER 2

Messages From The Angels

Divine Interventions Reiki Healing

A connection to spirit for a friend of the family.

RE: A message for my sister who reaches out to me for a friend of the family. Someone who has lost a loved one. I am asked to give a reading and I dream of those in spirit who step forward to give me messages for their loved ones. They appear before I am asked in the physical world to give messages or before I meet people, their spirit loved ones show themselves to me. I have a constant connection to the spirit realm. I talk all day with spirit. I dream about spirit and I basically live in amongst the worlds.

I pass on a reading to my sister Vicky, to give to her friend who has never been to a medium for a reading. Painful loses to the connections of people I have in this world. Spirit comes to me for I am open to their communication.

MESSAGE:

Jesse: Your mother stepped forward two days ago as I was driving to work. On the same street my niece Vanessa, stepped forward today. I receive the name; "Crystal" coming through two days ago. I pulled the wrong woman forward that day. It took me a little bit to know it was your mom. I saw your dad's face as I got your mother's name.

Your mom stepped forward and I missed it. There is always a message within a message in my writings. So please pay attention. Heed my words. Love comes forward in all the messages I receive.

"It has not always been a smooth ride for us."

Jesse: take what resonates with you. The rest may be for a future date. Your dad may have hidden messages in our communication today. Sometimes I have pushy angels.

"Down the line and over the fence they come." "Peeking in on you both".

I have a quote; *'Life's biggest tragedy is that we get old too fast and wise too late'.* By Benjamin Franklin

I have names that come together. Some may belong to you. Some may not make sense today. However, I am shown a line of women waiting in the wings for you. To support, love and nurture you.

They will bring you luck and good fortune. Connections always do.

"Benjamin" "Tina"

I receive the name 'jade', but I feel the energy behind the name. I feel it is foreign or the color is of significance to you or your family. The stone jade is powerful in your lineage or shortly in the distant land.

Saint Gabriel presents a 'moonstone' ring to me. The band is a rose gold in color. I see a million sparkles glowing from within this stone. I see pale colors. Pink, yellow, and purple are the colors that stand out to me.

I feel someone is reaching their hand out to show me this ring. I then see a purple stone. Maybe amethyst. There is a ring. Maybe two. I get the underlying message of the ring of angels and spirit that stand around you.

I see the flecks of glitter in between all these pale colors. Not everything is as it should be or appears to be in this world.

I see a magician.

I see a warrior and I feel the pain is remembered sometimes more than the good that we had.

"That hurts my heart".

"When I left it was not as bad as it seemed". I hear the words, "talk, talk, talk".

"'The mind chatters but the heart can't hear me". "The choice is easy once you let go".

I hear the song; "Tears from heaven". Please find it and listen with your heart.

"I will hold your hand and we can cry together". "Somethings to clear up and this will help".

Jesse: I woke this morning from a dream.

I stand in a field and the water is up around my ankles. I feel as though I stand in a rice patty. As I stand there I see the rain coming down hard all around me. *"Tears from heaven".*

Number 9- "Spirits a-plenty".

Message: Release any grudges or resentment you feel. Toward yourself or towards your loved ones. It was all so silly now that we look at it through the eyes from up here. We see today how it truly was. Holding onto these negative feelings only keeps holding us back.

"I could see you all this time. I felt your every pain. It's okay things turned out differently than we expected. There is a call to forgive and it starts with yourself. We all learn through our mistakes and you have done such a great job without me".

"Sit and talk with me. Remember if you can. Find the photo album somewhere in the back of your mind. I will help you pull out some memories of just yours and mine".

"Sit in silence in your car. I love the warmth and closeness I feel when I sit beside you while you drive. Turn on my favorite music. The 70's and 80's. I know it will be painful for you for your taste seems so different than mine. But I will come through. My spirit will soar, feel it and see it as I erupt through the music. Little words, hidden messages if you let me guide your heart and eyes to the songs I remember where mine".

Quote: All people were created the same. It is time for you to let go of any blame… Dad hidden message for you in this…

Whitney Houston: The movie 'Bodyguard'—*"I will always love you".* "Keep moving forward you deserve the best".

"You deserve to be happy".

"What's holding you back".

"You know what I'm talking about".

"She's beautiful and you know your heart best".

"No guilt and no remorse let go of me so you can love again fully".... "Protect yourself and all that's dear".

Jesse: "your my whole world no one will ever take your place in my heart". "Remember your magic". "Your beautiful". "I am so proud of all you are". *Jesse:* I have right eye pain.

"I see your dads pain. I feel it all the time. Nothing could have been done differently. My game had been won. Home is not always what we think it is. You're just here for a short while enjoy it. Live it up as best you can".

"I am like a mirror sometimes so close to you it hurts".

Jesse: "I want to touch you". "I want to hold you, but I need you to bring me in."

"You've changed and grown since the time I last held you". "You're a powerful woman and so strong in spite of it all."

"I see the lost boy in your dad".

"His world crashed in around him, but I never truly left his side."

"I push him and try to get him to see I am in a much better place now."

"My ashes need scattering so he can move on."

I hear, "Cross my heart, hope to cry, stick a needle in your eye". "Painful letting go but do it".

"It's painful to see you sometimes".

"Choices we make our health is the only thing we can control and yet we keep choosing all the bad things". "I guess it's just human nature". "WE LOVE YOU" !!!!!!!!!!

I see the infinity sign. To the right, to the left, to the bottom and to the top. I feel soldier energy as I write this. Military service. Angel's galore... ... ...

"These days are short". "The nights are long". "Use them to heal". "My warrior".

"My knight and shining armor".

"I've earned my wings and I can fly anywhere". "A house on the hill".

"A mansion in the sky". "I didn't need much to make me happy for you were the sunshine in my life."

"Record Keeper".

Jesse: I work with cards and I pull one from each deck. The universe sees your needs and I will give you what you need...

Animals are our strong connection to spirit. We all have them to help guide us through this painful world.

The turtle peeks its head out of her shell. "I see your every move". I feel this younger energy 30's maybe 40's.

Chameleon: The song by Boy 'George'.

Cards Message: Stay in the background and adapt to the situation rather than being conspicuous and attempting to direct the course of events.

Jesse: Is there a situation or 'by chance a change' you're trying to work through? A decision? A change of jobs or a move your contemplating?

Spirit gives me the less your worry about it the easier it will come. The answer has already been worked out in your mind. Just take a couple more days or months and it will be clearer.

The first card, I feel was the opposite of who you are. I feel you are a go-getter, and nothing can hold you back. Your spirit soar's every time you walk through a new door. "Keep it up baby girl".

"Your my trooper for sure". I feel grandfather energy with this message.

You easily adapt to change and go with the flow of life. That's the best way to look at life and it will help you succeed every time you belief you can, you do!!! Is there a "Patricia" in your family or outer circle?

Spiritual meaning of chameleon? Please research it.

Angel of Unity- Connecting back to family is important today.

"So many angels so little time". "Wonder Woman"....

"Rex".

"You're momma's hero"... ... ...

"Never doubt my presence always see the signs of me surrounding you".

2/6 numbers your mom wants me to see. Twenty-six is unity. "You and me together forever".

"Heart and soul honey, no matter what kept us down, it could never keep us apart." "I know you were tiny, and I was so tired".

"My super strength I got from you".

"Feel me, let me in and I will show you my presence. Let me touch you. If you will. A feather lite touch on your cheek or your arm. Feather's from heaven signs every day. Blue jay cries and I want you to see I try to speak to you. Your thoughts will awaken if you let them. Nature and the 'son' will revive us both".

"Bring me along and listen really close". "I will whisper on the wind and you can hear my songs of love reach your ears." I see the color blue. "Don't be sad anymore".

"Lift my heart off the floor".

I see a large angel. Wings of pure white. She spreads them in front of you. Your guardian angel Uriel the rays of red will show you when she is around.

"I will bring her to you." "You can be sure mom is with me each and every time".

I see a bright red silken gown. Like a kimono, one a Japanese woman may wear. I feel its beauty could never compare to the woman your mother sees within you. I see her hair all wrapped in a bun. "Tight and snug as a bug in a rug". Beautiful shiny black hair all atop your little head.

I'm being asked to gift you with a stone. A malachite stone. It's not jade but comes in a darker shade of green, the family tree in the distance. A connection and a love from your past. I will give it to my sister. Passing things down and letting go, so others can be happy.

Don't hang on to the past for it holds you back from your future.

"Rex and Jesse I love you and never forget; "I am only a whisper away".

"Vicky thank you for holding "our" man. I release him to you, now do with him what you can"!!

Messages from My Own Band of Angels

Finding the love and light in our lives sometimes can be a real challenge. For many of us, we struggle to get through life one day at a time or even one moment at time. God shares so much love and wisdom with me throughout the past five years. My inner voice has come to life and I come to understand the angels that walk with me, surround me and love me speak loud through my own heart. We play together as if we were children and so very young at heart some days.

In 2015 the Lord placed a sweet angel in my lap and asked me to walk with Him while He taught me what true love is. Little Miss Felicia is an angel who lost her voice and due to circumstances beyond her control found herself in Christ's arms in the heavens above. The Lord taught me that her death, like so many others has broken His heart. I record her case and a few others in the thirty-three books the Lord has asked me to write for Him. Without my special band of angels, I would not have been as strong today without the fun and laughter of their presence in my life.

I want to thank Robin Williams for he has helped me understand my own reality is much like his was. He ran with his own band of angels and I could see it when he was on stage. He was an amazing entertainer and comedian. God pulls Robin forward on this journey to help keep my heart light and full of love.

God tells me my life may have been different than Robin's; however, our souls are very similar. Full of love and laughter and Robin and I share God's light through all we do. Always bringing smiles to everyone in our life, no matter how the world affected us on the inside.

So, I want to thank my little friend, 'Mork", 'Na-nu, Na-nu"!!!

A little history on Robin Williams:

Mork, an alien from the planet Ork on a mission to Earth to study human behavior, travels to 1970's Boulder, Colorado, where he meets up with

Mindy, a young journalism graduate, after his egg-shaped spacecraft lands there. The bumbling alien is trying to get a handle on Earth culture and his frequent dispatches back to his home planet give him the opportunity to sound off on human foibles. This spinoff of "Happy Days" features Robin Williams as Mork in an early starring role for the comic actor. As Mork would say; "Na-nu, na-nu".

First episode date: September 14, 1978.

The first role I ever saw Robin Williams play in when I just a young girl. "Mork and Mindy". I learned to love Robin when I was only twelve-years old. Throughout the years; I only grew fonder of him. Now He lifts my spirits and I could never make up such beautiful bantering without this little guy showing himself, back down here on this earth plane.

I want to thank you Robin for making my housekeeping duties lighter, for I always pretend I am 'Mrs. Doubtfire' to make cleaning tasks go by much quicker. Dancing and twirling and singing, "Luck be a lady tonight".

One special night spent with Robin in the kitchen; Jesus and the angels flood my senses and Robin and I sing in the kitchen to "The Lost Boys". An amazing memory I will never forget. I cry tears and dance with my angels in the kitchen as Miss Felicia sits on the table dangling her feet clapping. A message from God; "I hope you are having the time of your life". As Robin Williams, in heaven steps forward to keep my heart light and full of joy. Special moments as he pops in and out my life to lift my spirits. All while I work taking care of God's special needs adults. Mentally and physically handicapped adults, one of the many jobs I have held over the years since God fully awakened me. Interior visions and the angels and I play together when we are alone.

Quote: Forgiveness is a conscious effort that should be worked on every day.

"Love is the answer".

3:11 a.m.

Winter of 2017

Too early in the morning and my angel brigade works through the night and into the early morning hours with me. As I wake to go to the bathroom I am asked to write this in my newest book.

Robin is pissed....

"Come on guys do we really have to do this"?

"It's too F&c(ing early for this s&it". Shrugging his shoulders and smiling as usual. Robin always likes to pop in to give me a hard time.

I hear him pop in and my eyes are not even open as I go to the bathroom this morning.

Whitney and Robin have been together for a while, in my angel brigade. She is constantly giving him a big push, just like Elaine on Seinfeld. Whitney Houston tries to keep Robin Williams in line, and she is unsuccessful most of the time.

As I wake I am asked to share the song of the morning: *"Love is the answer"*-by Tanya Tucker.

June and Johnny Cash are the stand-ins for Tanya this morning in my line-up of angels. This song rolls through my consciousness as Robin steps into the picture so early this morning.

I hear; "I love you more today, than I did yesterday".

"Love is the answer". "Love is the answer".

I saw Tanya Tucker in concert once when I was just out of high school. One of my favorite singers growing up. It was the week of Halloween and she came out onto stage wearing a black wig. She surprised the whole audience.

Her song, Love is the answer; is a message so early this morning as Robin wakes me as I go to the bathroom.

As I sit to turn on the computer, Robin chimes in; "Shouldn't we sing Happy Birthday to your ex"?

I roll my eyes as the computer comes on and the date flashes on the screen. December 5th is my ex-husbands birthday and the angels know it.

In frustration and sheer joy, I think to myself; "Really". "Lol".

I never know what the angels will bring forward, I just learn I don't walk alone, and I try to understand all the antics as we play together.

Thank you Robin and Whitney for this journey recording God's broken heart would not be nearly as easy without you popping in and out keeping my heart light in between all the lessons of darkness in my life and in this world.

I'm going back to bed and I pray for a miracle to be left alone for a few more hours!

Strange Bed Fellows

"Wow". "It's been so long since you said, "hello". (from Mrs. Doubtfire)… I hear Robin step forward.

"Good morning, Vietnam"…

"Where to h&ll have you been?"

Robin's back. He plays with me throughout the day…

I'm cooking dinner tonight and Robin shows up again. More love and laughter from the other side.

I have a little tiff with Jesus and Robin steps in to lighten the energy in the room. He tries to lift my spirits.

"Beans, beans the magical fruit the more you eat the more you toot". "The more you toot the better you feel, then you're ready for another meal". Robin sings this song to me as he stands over my right shoulder at the stove in the kitchen at work.

All in unison, they sing over and over. I hear my band of angels chime in on this song, as I try to work through some emotions as I have just had a disagreement with Jesus.

"They sound like a bunch of drunkasauruses". Liz Taylor pipes in.

Robin pipes in as he leans in too close. He takes a big whiff of my perfume. "Man, you smell like Liz". "Hmmmm".

The angels know I wear 'diamonds'. Liz Taylor's perfume and Robin's so close he can smell my perfume. He makes jokes and continues to blow my mind with his presence in my life.

Jesus sits in the background, in the kitchen and shakes His head and smiles, to see the band of angels that grace me after our little fight tonight.

Liz jokes with Jesus and tells Him; "she certainly is a talented little hothead". "Trying to save the world and writing love letters for you". "I'd say she missed her calling a few times, honey".

I see Liz and she wears a black dress that fits tight around her bosom. She wears a single strand of white pearls around her neck and she smokes a long cigarette with a plastic extension on the end of her cigarette. Elizabeth Taylor is regal and beautiful as ever tonight.

Interior visions that become my reality as the Lord walks with me daily.

God's grace truly is amazing.

"Michael Jackson is in the house". Robin introduces Michael and I warm my tea while I cook dinner.

Michael Jackson usually shows up when I need to dance. Dancing to music releases negative energy and the Lord sees I need to lift my spirits tonight, so I am allowed to see and play with my angels before I retire for the night.

"Hey, what about those strange bedfellows of yours"" Robin pipes in.

Robin reminds me we are never left alone. A knowing of what goes on in my world and the angels make up who I am is the underlying message with Robin's statement of 'strange bed fellows'.

Robin Williams comes in wearing a black and white stripped referees outfit. Trying to keep the peace between Jesus and me. I see the reference with the referees outfit. He brings out a white flag and he waves it in between Jesus and me. As I learn all of the angels that surround me, I learn Robin Williams is my inner child's playmate.

Robin shows up at church one day as a single white rabbit. Tricks God pulls out of His top hat for me and I am blessed the rest of my days. All the visions, dreams and experiences in my life come to be, because of the power of Jesus Christ in my life.

Robin shows up at church one morning and he is a single white rabbit. I see with my spiritual eye, as he hop's on the church floor and then turns into a little boy. I see his brown hair and a stripped blue and green short-sleeved shirt. He wears brown corduroy pants and white saddle shoes. He has one large red bulb on his nose just like in the "Patch Adam's" movie. He rides around in the middle of the church floor and then I see a hundred little rabbits come into the view of my spiritual eye. The small white rabbits are in representation of the little angels, Robin plays with the little children now he is on the other side. He raises my spirits and he keeps fun and laughter alive on the other side at the same time.

Robin shares a joke with me; and I am not sure if this is a known joke he shared while on stage or not.

Setting the scene:

Jesus stands with Robin as this joke comes through the veil. I stand among many great angels and this joke touches base on what the real world is like, on the outside skirts of my own reality. One I try to let God handle as much as I can.

So, Robin gives me a joke from the other side.

He shows me Estelle Getty stands with him and Jesus Christ in the middle of the courthouse floor. Estelle Getty's from the Golden Girls, she pipes in.

She steps forward; Estelle is dressed in an evening gown with golden sequins. She speaks; "Picture it, earth 2017".

Robin pipes in, "Picture this, the world as you live in it".

He shows me a vision as he waves his hand to the left. I see the chaos on the outside world as Robin reminds me in this vision, of what goes on outside my own reality with the Lord.

Robin speaks; "You have a panel of judges". Robin waves his hand out and he shows me a line of judges as if on the bench in a courthouse setting.

"You have a bunch of Cardinals and Priests". They are present in the courthouse with this panel of judges. They sit in the hot seat, so to speak. Robins hand waves out again and the Cardinals and Priests appear after he waves his hand again.

"You have a bunch of money hungry, over-bearing, egotistical government officials". They gather in the courthouse all of them.

I come to understand this as the days of God's judgement is being portrayed in this playful skit.

Robin continues: You have the scene of the Judges, Cardinals, Priests and the Government Officials all lined up in the courtroom. Robin then says; "Then you have Jesus Christ standing in the middle of the floor".

I see Robin, Jesus and Estelle Getty's standing in the middle of the courthouse floor, surrounded by the judges on their bench seats, the priests and cardinals and the government officials await judgement.

Again, Robin repeats; "You have a panel of judges, cardinals, priests and government officials and you have Jesus Christ standing in the middle."

Robin asks; "What do you have"?

A big smile on his face.

"You have all Hell breaking loose"!!

Then I get the famous, "Bada Bing", "Bada Boom". James Gandolfini (from the Soprano's, the mob boss) is on the drums in the darkened background.

"God is in the house"!! Robin pipes in and then he turns into the genie from Aladdin. He smiles and flies around the room and there are red arrow signs and he points at my head, feet, and belly. He lights up red arrows all around me. Making fun of me for I can't escape this tirade of band of angels. They all laugh it up as Robin and the gang drive me crazy.

I see Jesus as He sits in His throne. A very smug grin on His face and I see the love He holds for me in His eyes.

Ribbing and roasting from the other side and my reality is revealed in this entry. Playful bantering in between all the sad love stories I have written in our books over the past six years.

THE LORD STANDS WITH MOTHER TERESA

Quote: *Be faithful in small things because it is in them that your strength lies.*

March 11, 2019

6:00 a.m.

I am woken this morning and I hear a sweet voice. "Please pray for me".

I did not see who this was. I just heard the pain behind her voice.

A few minutes later, I see Mother Teresa of Calcutta. She kneels before me and I see her this time. She is in her white robe with the thin blue trim. She is kneeling and I see the left side of her face. She is so beautiful. She is young and no longer aged as I remember her. This is the first time I have seen her so beautiful.

She is praying and as she does, she tells me; "Prayer is an obligation".

Jesus reminds me of my visit with Father M. and I turn over and ask for strength from Mother Teresa. I ask for guidance with my words for sometimes I truly don't know why I meet with Father M. at the Catholic Church. I have been receiving counsel with him since August of 2016. One year after I started recording God's messages and warnings for the children of the world. I feel as if I am going nowhere. Jesus reminds me; *"All in good time".*

"My plan will be revealed".

I hold onto hope again this morning that I may be able to touch Father M.'s heart. I hold onto hope that he might step forward and speak to Monsignor D. or Bishop D. I hold onto hope for Christ's sake.

As I pray this morning I see the manger with the infant Jesus in it. It is on fire. My heart hurts and I know the significance with this vision. Christ's heart is truly broken for the children of this world. We discussed yesterday the fact that so many don't even have a chance at life right from the beginning. The suffering for the little children around the world does not go unnoticed by Abba; Our Father or Jesus Christ.

My knowledge comes straight from the Father now. Jesus and I walk hand in hand every step of the way. His love for me is very precious. Never could I have imagined such a beautiful connection with Him.

Jesus reminds me; *"I have exposed Myself to you"*.

6:00 p.m.

March 8, 2019

I wake up daily with Jesus Christ. He smiles with love in His eyes this morning. I hear the words;

"I love you meme". These words come from my grandson who is just waking up beside me. Never a more precious moment than to lay with my two favorite guys this morning.

Curtis and I get up to go to church this morning. Jesus is so proud of me for all I have come to accept. My new life. My new love and my heart beats strong with Abba's daily. We are one in the Holy Spirit. I see Them. I feel Them. I know of Their Presence every second of the day.

My grandson met Father M. today, three days before I meet with him for counseling.

Jesus prepares me for my meeting with Father M. and I still am not sure what we will discuss on Monday. So many visions and too many lessons to record.

I will be taking my grandson to church for the first time today and it is a lesson for me of how precious it is when a child of God learns of Christ's passionate love for them.

I see God at work every day. He is pushing me through the doors of the Catholic Church with our love story. A gift for me and Mother Mary. A gift for the Catholic Church. A gift for my own children. I have been granted with Divine Mercy and God wants this love story shared with the children of the world.

March 3, 2019

I feel the cross covering my left eye. I see the pain it has brought to Jesus' heart. I see the pain and know daily God see's every single cross, every single child carries. I feel His pain with this knowing. I feel it within my heart. I feel it through my body and manifestations of my body.

As I feel the pain in my left eye. I feel the shape of the cross covering my eye. It's as if He has set the cross over my left eye lid this morning.

As I sit in church this morning at Saint John's I see God's fist. It is solid gold and it comes straight down in front of me. It comes in straight from the Heavens above this morning. I see God everywhere I go. He speaks to my heart with everyone I meet. I listen, I learn, and I know of His presence with me and within them. His messages never go unnoticed.

The fist I see comes in suddenly. It is solid gold. God reminds me of the vision of His hand reaching down to Adam. Not nearly as powerful as the golden fist He has shown me this morning.

I prepare for Lent this morning and finally after fifty-one years I get the meaning behind the preparation of the days before this beautiful season. The thirty-three days of consecration and now I know; why God works so tirelessly to teach me. The Catholic Church is so special to Him.

Honoring and loving Jesus Christ, the sacraments, the commandments, the Bible and Christ's sacrifice is remembered with such reverence; it is all so beautiful.

As I walk today, I see the largest orb just to the left of me. I see it as big a bubble. It is almost the size of a volleyball. Inside there are the electric currents that are like lightning strikes within it.

God shares with me this is Mother Mary's presence. She walks just in front of me now. I follow in her footsteps so closely; I don't see her.

God continues to place her crown on my head. I tell Him; "I don't want a crown." I tell Him; "I want to help Your Sacred Heart beat stronger".

"I want to speak of Your broken heart".

"I want to speak of my truth and knowing of Your love for all the little children". "I want to share with the world, Your Divine Mercy".

"I want to share with the world, the love You have showered down upon me".

Vision: I stand under Christ's cross and the blood and water pours out of Jesus' wound at His side. I drink of the blood and water. Christ has poured His Mercies down upon me. His Mercy is great with this vision. His love for me is shown to me over my entire life, as He walks with me and reminds me of who He created me to be.

I see in this vision and I kneel in front of the Lord as He hangs from the cross. I open my mouth wide and receive His words of Mercy. I receive His love as I accept all He teaches me. Jesus shows me Abba's love for me with all the messages and knowing of my true death.

I see the Lord shows me, coming out from under His Sari (robe). I am a young child in this vision. He opens His Sari and I come out from beneath His robe.

As I lay down this morning after my walk, I see the dragon just in front of me. God tells me I have faced all my fears head on. Nothing will stop His love for me from becoming all He has shown me.

We make plans to go to church more often. We make plans for a retreat. We make plans to become Christ's bride in the eyes of the Catholic Church.

Vision: I see Juan Diego and I see Our Lady of Guadeloupe. I see my skin. I see my skin on the material that is behind Our Lady of Guadeloupe. My own life, my own sacrifice. My own love for Jesus Christ. The Mother of God and Abba continues to show me at the foot of Our Father. I am continually shown; me at the foot of the Tree of Knowledge. I am shown me sitting at the end of the Last Supper Table at the opposite end of Jesus Christ. God shows me, I sit at the foot of His Throne. God the Father teaches me, of His great love for me.

God teaches me of my own resurrected body, heart and soul. He continues to tell me I am a gift back to the Catholic Church.

Two days this week I see statues of Mother Mary and they are in ashes. The remnants of her burnt offerings for Christ's love.

Vision: I see myself as Mary holding Jesus after He was taken down from the cross. I am covered in His blood. Tears flowing from my eyes. I feel the thorns pierce my tender heart, as His crown is wrapped around my bleeding heart today.

I repeat the words; *"What have they done to you"*? I repeat these words, over and over as my heart feels so much pain.

These are painful visions, memories and knowing. It has become my reality.

God tells me; *"You are my burning bush".*

Abba continues to tell me, *"You are My Truest Light"*. *"From the beginning to the end"*.

March 10, 2019: At mass I hear her. Saint Margarette Mary. She speaks in French and I try to understand her. I don't know what she is speaking I just know she is there.

I wait and then I hear these words; "His love for you goes beyond this world".

God's speaks the word; *"Ardent Receptivity"*- open and responsive to ideas and impressions, fit to receive and transmit stimuli.

CHAPTER 3

Dreamtime

Mother Mary wakes me:

At 1:11 a.m. on February 17, 2021 I wake to the "Vital Grace of God". I feel Mother Mary and she vibrates me awake. I recognize her soul awakens within me this morning. Her Holy Presence has come to life within me. My true death experience was real, and she reminds me of that, this morning. The knowledge of my own crossing has been explained to me many times over the course of this journey since March of 2012. Never a more powerful presence than to be woken by Our Father, Jesus Christ and Mother Mary.

Our hearts are connected from the beginning of time to the ends of all time.

Mother Mary shares with me a visual of my granddaughter Lovis. A pure soul through and through. She is only eight months old and she is growing fast. Mother Mary takes me back to her birth which was ten days prior to my birthday. July 11th, 2020 was Lovis' birth date. In my communication and learning signs and symbols I find the number eleven means "open doorways". As the Lord promises me movies, documentaries and doors are opening daily, I come to see how beautiful it is to be alive this morning. The presence of my creator wakes me.

Like so many other times over the past five years. A powerful experience and I come to understand so much through my heart connection to Mother Mary. A reality many would never understand. A reality many will judge me as losing my mind.

I wake to the song from Adele's twenty-one album. Twenty-one was the day I was born. July 21, 1967. 10 days after my granddaughter's birth-day. Adele's album 21 is one I have found strength in listening to, as I came through my spiritual emergence. Uplifting messages in Adele's powerful songs. Connections in my heart back to the cross at Calvary come through in her messages within the lyrics.

Song of the morning: *Love Song*

Love Song

Whenever I'm alone with you
You make me feel like I am home again
Whenever I'm alone with you
You make me feel like I am whole again
Whenever I'm alone with you
You make me feel like I am young again

Mother Mary brings forward this special song and then shows me my granddaughter for a reason. During the pandemic little Lovis was born at home. During the pandemic of 2020, she entered this world with the assistance of her father, Joe. My daughter Sherri set up a birthing pool in her living room in her apartment. Her son Curtis was upstairs sleeping. My daughter is an amazing woman and mother. She has grown into a powerful teacher, talented artist and an amazing mother. After her son's birth I find Sherri's extraordinary gifts and talents lie within her. Not all of them have been discovered yet. Curtis was diagnosed with Autism early in his life.

Something that seems to be so prevalent today. Sherri's mothering skills excel the ones I feel I had. I see such a loving, giving and compassionate mother come to life within her. Her patience is beyond a saint's. She has natural knowledge of how to handle every situation that comes forward in her life with Curtis and Lovis. I am so proud of the woman she has become.

On the outskirts of my own little world, I see a women's movement occurring and my generation and Sherri's generation are learning to stand tall and proud. We seem to come from broken women, yet I know from my own family history, we come from strong stalk and powerful lineage. Pushing through many challenges over the years. My grandmother raised eleven children by herself back during the depression. The depression ran from August 1929 to March of 1933. It was a time in history that changed the world. This event in history sent Wall Street into a panic and wiped out millions of investors.

Consumer spending and investments dropped, causing steep declines in industrial output and employment as falling companies laid off workers.

My grandmother survived abuses I couldn't even imagine. I have heard horror stories and today I see just were all that abuse and shameful behavior has led this generation of women. It has risen them up and made them strong leaders and powerful entrepreneurs.

My daughter's circumstances and choices have led her and formed her life into something beautiful. She is a stay at home mother. Her world came to a halt the day her son was born. Unexpectedly he was born with a cyst in his throat and was a high medical needs child from birth. Unable to breath on his own when he came into this world. He was rushed from one hospital to another by life flight helicopter. In less than 24-hours he was prepped for surgery and his rough journey was well underway. I call Curtis *Meme's little hero'*. He is a brave warrior for coming into this world. He is a strong tiger for all he has survived up to this point in his life. He is only six years old. I pray for strength of his mother to be passed down to him. I pray that the intelligence I see bursting through his little world, is shared some day with many. Curtis has taught me what true love is. He has taught me what strength and perseverance is and he has taught me that the pure love of God shines out through his little heart and soul.

Lovis and Curtis are only a glimpse into the love I have created and helped nourish in this life. I have two boys and five other grandchildren. All on different paths and all with similar challenges and struggles ahead of them. I don't get to see them nearly as often as I would like and that's a huge lesson today as God has put the brakes on this world. Using the darkness to bring His light back into the world, is what I understand this pandemic to be. I pray daily for God to help bring a healthier and more vital human race to the forefront after this pandemic subsides and heals a hurt world. I hope that unity comes to the forefront for we surely need all the miracles in the world, to shine through all the darkness.

Mother Mary made a choice a long time ago and that was to bring the Messiah into this world. A miracle and legacy Jesus Christ has helped many generations learn the true value of family. He helped millions and even billions of people over the years come to understand their own cross.

There are so many people today that are not fully awakened to the message Jesus brought into the world. He brought the Law of Love into the world. After so much pain, suffering and hate was spread since the beginning of time, Jesus Christ was teaching us God's Word and Greatest Law is and will always be, to LOVE.

No rules or laws are greater in the book of knowledge. No man has touched, changed or shifted the worlds outcome more profoundly than Jesus Christ. I walk daily with the Savior of the world. He leads me in love every day and yesterday as I prepared to assist and aid my oldest sister Vicky with healing of the mind, body and spirit I was given a phrase. As I walk out of the shower and dry off the Lord and I converse, and we joke and play all day long. Christ literally has come to life within me. My very spirit is lifted up by the Lord and the angels that surround me. As I dry off Jesus speaks; *"Strip me naked and call me Jesus"*. A joke the Lord brings forward as we stand with Robin Williams, a special connection I have with the spirit realm. I never walk alone. The angels swoop in and keep my life full of laughter. I could not stop laughing for a few moments afterward. As the words sunk in I was shown Jesus on the cross. Over 2,000 years ago the Greatest Man to walk the face of the earth was hung from a cross. He was tortured immensely before many of His own followers. He was tortured before His own mother. The very heart and soul of our Creator was tortured and killed on a cross. The most beautiful sacrifice for us, was Jesus Christ on the cross. He hung from the cross to teach us what pure love is.

Jesus Christ's birth, His walk with the cross in the wilderness and His death; was a beautiful symbol of Our Heavenly Father's Pure Love for humanity.

Many religions have been formed and created since the beginning of time as we know it. Some forced upon other cultures and races. Many rites and rituals have been changed and laws and regulations put into place. We humans try desperately to do things 'right'. We try to do things by the book. I ask when did it become so difficult that we forgot the greatest law of life? When did we forget the simplest law of life?

Loving doesn't have to be so difficult. It should come naturally to us all.

Ego and fear are our own worst enemy in this world. Something that leads to a wounded soul and then snowballs into pained hearts and even hatred. As the Mother of God wakes me this morning she reminds me of Adele's Love Song. Our Heavenly Mother reminds me of the pure innocent love of Lovis and Curtis. She reminds me of simpler times in history. Mother Mary reminds me of how things used to be. When the world didn't seem so painful.

Mother Mary brings forward to my spiritual eye as I lay with her vibrating within me, this very powerful song. She shows me Curtis and Lovis and how different their skin color is. The heritage and background just the color of their skin brings out. Curtis has English/French, black heritage, and Cherokee blood running through his veins. Lovis on the other hand is pure lily white. To see them together with Curtis holding his baby sister hurts the eyes. I see such love between these two children and the reality of what has been going on in this world, is so heartbreaking. Mother Mary tells me these two children's love story would break the hearts of millions if it came to light in the world. Extraordinary children are born every day. To me these two are not just one in a million. They are the center in my very heart and soul. They are the future of this world. They are meant for great things. I hope this morning, after being woken by my heavenly mother, that Jesus Christ's promise and law of love will outshine all the darkness that seems to creep its way above all the light that is in God's world.

Just a snippet into my world as Mother Mary wakes me at 1:11 a.m. this morning.

I am reminded by the Lord of the bruise in the crook of my right arm. A bruise I have no idea how it got there. I look down at it and He reminds me of the time early on in my spiritual emergence of the day my daughter and I went to donate blood. I was ungrounded and having a hard time wanting to stay in this world. I was living and creating chaos in my life. I was trying to be too many things to all the people in my life. I was running myself ragged. I was being called by God to slow down!

As I lay on the table to give blood back in 2006, to help someone in need of a lifesaving transfusion, I am experiencing what I call a bleed through. A memory or event that I was unaware of that was deeply imbedded in my soul. I had the feeling and sense of being on the cross back at Calvary. My duel reality was coming to the forefront on the table at the red cross center back in 2006, just before I had my first break down. Jesus brings this memory to the forefront yesterday as I see a bruise in the crook of my arm where a needle would be placed to give blood.

As I lay on the table with my arms outstretched as if on the cross, while the woman drawing blood tightens the strap around my right arm, I feel sick to my stomach. I start to sweat, and I have a flashback. A memory. I see myself, as Jesus on the cross at Calvary. Hung above the dark soil. I see the rocky ground beneath my feet, and I feel the agonizing pain of the spikes in my feet. The spikes in my hands are torturous, yet the pain that will never be released from me, I feel is the crown of thorns around my delicate head. A meaning and a message coming through as I am aware of the torture of so many souls over the years with mental illness.

This was a very painful time in my life. Back in the year, 2006 I wanted to exit this world. I wanted to die. God was calling out to me to slow down. He has reached out to me many times over the years. Finally; after my NDE He fully got my attention.

The spiritual emergence that was happening ended up driving me into a spiritual emergency, this is what lead to my diagnosis of 'Bipolar II' and then in 2007 my 'Bipolar I' diagnosis and in 2014 with my diagnosis 'Bipolar I with PTSD'. All labels on a piece of paper that did not define the battles I was fighting or the fact I was being called to wake up to more than what the human mind can comprehend.

Hidden messages were coming through the veil. I started my awakening. I have a heart connection and love for Jesus Christ and His mother, one that I still don't fully understand. I just write and love Him through the typewritten word. Messages come to me and I experience a profound love from the spirit world. Something I hope to share with others. We do not walk alone. None of us are crazy. We are AWAKENING!!

After living in the darkness, with myself for such a long time I find my truth by the lamp the Lord has shining at my feet. He lights up all my truths. Thirty-four years later I find taking care of the elderly has been an extremely rewarding job. I feel in my very soul, it is time to open new doors and move into something even more beautiful. As my writing career is surely to take off soon. I shift gears and open the Holistic Health and Healing Center. The center Jesus Christ asked me to raise money for nearly five years ago. A calling within a calling just like Mother Teresa.

Mother Mary brings forward, *"You are the woman"*. *"The Sign of the Sun"*. She reminds me of another vision. A time I sat at a red light. Stopped on Stillwater ave. waiting for time to pass while I listened to the Lord remind me of who I am, God share with me this vision. I see a black circle around the sun in the sky. As I sit and converse with the Lord, the circle and the sun dance in the sky. In a circular motion it moves. I am crying as this happens. I am trying to work through the message and love that I am being shown in this very moment. The sun becomes stronger and moves closer. It continues to move in a circular motion. A vision buried deep within the thirty-three books I have written, and no one has seen them, but the Catholic Church.

A message and a warning and now they are lost inside a plethora of books written. God bears His soul to me.

History in the making:

Since March 21, 2020:

27.8 million cases of COVID-19 have been recorded. 488,000 deaths have occurred in the United States of America along. Worldwide the numbers are staggering. 109 million cases recorded.

2.42 million deaths and 61.6 million children of God have recovered from this horrible disease.

In history it was recorded in the year 1918 the pandemic (H1N1 virus) it lasted from 1918-1919, also called the Spanish Flu, lasted between one and two years. The pandemic occurred in three waves, though not simultaneously around the globe. It is estimated that about 500 million people or one-third of the world's population became infected with this virus. The estimated number of deaths was estimated to be at least 50 million worldwide with about 675,000 deaths occurring in the United States alone.

Historians now believe that the fatal severity of the Spanish flu's second wave was caused by the mutated virus spread by wartime troop movements. When the Spanish flu first appeared in early March of 1918, it had all the hallmarks of a seasonal flu, albeit a highly contagious and virulent strain.

The Lord shines light into the darkened world during a time in history where so much history is being brought to the surface. God makes history and He creates history. He is the Great Writer of all life's stories.

In History what is the sign of the sun?

The Miracle of the Sun (Portugal Milagre do Sol), also known as the Miracle of Fatima, is a series of events reported to have occurred miraculously on 13 October, attended by a large crowd who Gathered in Fatima, Portugal, in response to a prophecy made by three shepherd children, Lucia, Santos, and Francisco…

The oldest girl, Lucia was the only one to speak to her, and Mary told the children that she would reappear to them on the thirteenth day of the following months. She then vanished.

Connections from the past so we can all have hope for the future. That is what the Lady of the Sun is all about. Mother Mary has stepped forward in big ways throughout history. The Mother of God bringing light to this world, time and time again.

Today she enlightens us of her knowledge of Jesus Christ's needs. I have written His needs for the children of the world. A gift and a message of warnings for the past five plus years.

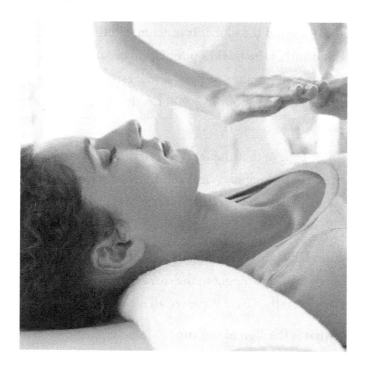

I opened our first studio for Reiki energy healing back in February of last year. One month later the doors were shut because of COVID-19 and the pandemic was in full swing. An expensive venture and journey as the Lord shows me door after door on this walk. I continue to wait for Him to open the right doors. I wait for the abundance of help He promises me will come. I wait for someone to recognize His pleas for help, for the children of the world.

I have moved seven times in the past ten years. A hard way to find where your soul can nurture itself and grow when you feel your feet aren't planted anywhere secure. One month ago, I moved into an apartment of my own. A most beautiful little space to call my own. I have come to love the quiet and peace it brings to my heart.

Growing my energy healing business and continuing with my writing and sharing my story of survival has become my new passion. The Lord is bringing clients to me. Four clients in just one week. A special plan I feel unfolding finally as I continue to follow the Lord's breath. I listen daily to His Words. I read bits and pieces from the Bible. I pray and meditate, and I attend church as often as I can.

I will be sharing stories of the special people God has placed in my life. Some will come briefly and go on their way. Some will stay and help me grow as I aid and assist them on their own journey.

The woman I am about to share part of her journey and love with you, God put her into my life nearly three and half years ago. I had moved from a bad relationship with a man who needs much spiritual growth. A man who struggles with 'mommy' issues. He does not comprehend what self-love or self-respect is. A man that suffers with prejudices and his mother drove a wedge between us and she had a hard time letting go of the apron strings she had wrapped around his waist. After seven years, I left this relationship to find peace in my heart, yet again with the Lord.

Moving forward and moving on is what we are asked to do today. Don't let anything hold you back from being the best you, you can be. As I learn and grow my client and friend Betty reaches out to me for a Reiki energy healing session. I observe Betty when she first walks through the door. Her emotions are close to the surface. She needs mentoring and a safe place to open her heart and let the tears flow. I provide my clients with just that. A calming environment and a soothing place to rest their head.

As Betty arrives and we stand face to face. (six feet apart of course and wearing our facemasks). I feel one all over body chill. The angel's greeting me and thanking me for helping Betty today. I have come to understand the spirit world knows before we do what we are going to do and the time frame in which it will occur. The angels nudging and prompting us is what I have come to understand. I met Betty's family in the spirit world before I met Betty. I receive names and sometimes it can be difficult because the angel brigade that walks with me is huge. After my crossing over experience I recognized nearly one-hundred fifty angels present and around me. It was hard to place who was stepping forward and who a message was for in the beginning of my communication.

When I feel the bone chilling touch of the angels go up and down my whole body I smile and tell Betty; "Your family is here, and they just gave me a hug for you". I feel, see, hear and smell things. My knowing is only what God will allow me to know. My senses are awakened. I pass along what information comes in and then let the client decide what belongs to her and what it may mean to her later.

COVID-19 has changed the way I run my business. I have certain criteria I have set in place for the clients safety and for my own safety. After the routine check in is done, paperwork signed, Betty and I move into the healing room. I work with Betty with centering and calling in her angels, doctors, and healers. I then call in my own. I ask for assistance from source energy light to help Betty today. I ask for Jesus to guide my hands and assist Betty with her healing session. I ask for Mikao Usui (the founder of Reiki) to assist us today.

Betty laid on the Reiki table and I placed a meditation pillow over her eyes so she could focus within. I placed an amethyst stone on her third eye, to open her all-knowing seeing eye, for clearer sight. I placed a sodalite stone on her throat chakra for assistance in opening her throat chakra so she may express herself more clearly and find her voice. Green aventurine was placed on her heart chakra, which is on the front of her chest, over her heart area. This will open Betty's heart to the light of God so she may receive healing and love. It will allow love to flow in and out. It will assist releasing some of her pain. Orange calcite is placed on Betty's sacral chakra and at her root chakra is a multi-faceted garnet. For cleansing and releasing old wounds of the feminine and reproductive system. All stones used to aid Betty in opening, cleansing and clearing her chakra system as Betty allows herself to align, mind, body and spirit. She uses deep cleansing breaths to aid and assist with the flow of Qi (lifeforce energy within) to flow throughout her body. In to receive love out to cleanse and rid the body of negative energy and toxins.

At the beginning of the session I used sage for smudging and clearing Betty's aura. Ridding her of negative energy around her as I have been taught by 'Great Spirit' on this journey.

I have worked with the Lakota's on this journey. Those in spirit. Hearing them call my soul and teaching me the importance of rituals has been so beneficial as I learn to be my own shaman.

Reiki energy healing invoked. Qi awakened within me to help aid Betty and sent with the intention of healing. One natural healing modality that worked wonders for me as I walked through some very dark times during my spiritual emergence and the awakening.

I worked with channeling healing love and light today with Betty. As I assisted Betty in grounding at the end of her session I receive the following vision. As I hold Betty's feet I ask her to envision large roots coming from her feet. I ask her to envision these roots going into the ground and securing her to mother earth. As I hold space for Betty and assist her in grounding, I see a large oak tree. I understand the oak tree to hold the meaning of 'strength' at the root starts when we open to self-love and self-healing.

I was given the message of Betty's twin sister, Sarah Ann who is in the spirit world, would like Betty to find a tree in her favorite park and come sit with her and talk. I saw Sarah Ann beneath this tree. She is waiting for Betty to come to her.

Sarah Ann shared with me Betty gives too much of herself to others and it is time for her to start taking care of herself.

Sarah Ann reminded me that Betty and she are 'soulmates'. Sarah Ann is a twin that Betty's mother lost during her pregnancy. In a private reading I connected to Sarah Ann and was given her name by her grandmother. Who Sarah Ann was named after by the spirit world and her loved ones. Something I found out when a baby is lost due to miscarriage or an abortion, those in the spirit world will name the souls of those lost. All souls are accounted for in the House of the Lord.

I received the message; 'Betty needs to find her voice and stand up more for herself'.

I suggested after Betty's healing session to do a cleansing of her aura daily with sage or palo santo's.

I also received the message; 'Hannah is one of Betty's guardian angels'. She asks Betty to call on her for protection, guidance and love on her daily walks.

Betty shares with me in our daily connection, that the cardinal bird is her spirit animal. Betty has many sightings and appearances of the cardinal bird in her life. The angels appear through the nature of God if we pay attention.

CHAPTER 4

Lost Soul Spirit Connections

*CASES AND EXPERIENCES BROUGHT TO ME AS THE LORD
DIRECTS ME TO ASSIST OTHERS WITH THE SPIRITUAL
WARFARE IN THIS WORLD...*

Releasing Robin

Back in October of 2015 I was handed by the Lord a sweet angel. Her love story God will never forget. The reason I write is for the children who do not have a voice. Children who have suffered and wish only to be loved.

The largest missing child's case in Maine. The Lord placed this sweet angel in my lap, and He asked me to walk with Him while He helped me understand God the Father's broken heart. I was asked to listen and to open my heart to a world full of spirit. Learning to see beyond the veil is what Jesus Christ has taught me. He showed me the science behind human beings. He showed me the energy you put into this world is the energy you will get out of it.

Jesus Christ opened a whole new world for me on October 29, 2015. My first real case study was a woman who had attached herself to my nephew. A ghost's energy. A spirit or entity. Her spirit and soul was stuck in this world, for the pain she had experienced wouldn't allow her to ascend to be in the higher realms. It wouldn't allow her soul to be with her children in the higher planes. A woman who suffered greatly before she died of cancer and lost her very heart when all three of her children died in a house fire.

Lost Soul Spirit Connections- Case #1

Message: "I will know what I know when I know it". "Not one second beforehand".

Messages from the spirit world come to us in all ways. The six senses teach us many things. Our sight teaches us to see. When we close our eyes, we can experience magic. We can dream and we can visualize. I see best sometimes when my eyes are closed. Spirit will appear and show themselves to me. I however; need to watch for the signs the angels will place before me and that is what I have done. This project allowed me to see how the angels that we cannot always see, will work in the physical world and put before us, messages and signs of what is to come. They will aid and assist us if we pay attention.

Smell, sight, touch, taste, sound and the knowing all go hand in hand when it comes to being in tune with your intuition and senses. The following occurs and I learn how to communicate to that which we can't always see with our physical eyes.

Signs and Symbols

Lance comes to me. First sound vibrations. Dogs barking, crunching leaves, car alarms and gun shots. I hear this as a message coming in through the veil. I have learned how to pick up on the waves of my deceased spirit family and friends. They talk to me through everything.

I see a dime on the ground. It is face up. The dime has a hole in it in the shape of a leaf. A tiny little hole in the dime and it represents and gives me a message, if I pay attention. On the back side is the identical leaf shaped hole, only slightly higher. It represents on one side, the high side on the other side the low side. Dark and light, maybe is the message. The hole in this dime being in the shape of a leaf, I recognize as being odd. It is a sign and a message. 'Pennie's from heaven' is a sign from your angels, that they are around. Today I receive the knowing of ten angels or more. I am being asked to pay attention.

It takes several days for the message to click. I have help from Ashley, my son's girlfriend. She is a very intuitive woman. She has had her gifts of seeing and knowing of spirit since she was a child. She is a gifted seer and a loving child of God.

I have trouble seeing spirit, but Ashley has had her gifts since she was ten years old. I see her at my daughter's apartment, and she asks me; "who is the guy in the red shirt with black pants"? She knows it has to do with me. I breathe in a cleansing breathe and think. I ask her to tell me all she sees. As she continues to talk I know it is my friend Lance. I ask Ashley to give me his name. She gets nothing. I asked for a letter. She give me the letter 'L'. I think Laura at first. I am always doubting myself with what information is coming in. The Lord tells me; "It is Lance". My childhood friend, my first crush. The boy I lost to a hunting accident when he was fifteen. Lance passed from a gunshot wound to his femur. He bled out in the woods while waiting for the rescue crew to get to him in the backwoods behind my grandfather's old property. I was only nine or ten years old. Lance was the first death I had ever experienced. A very painful loss for me and at such a tender age.

The red shirt represents the blood shed of my friend Lance. The black pants represents his leg wound which killed him. Black represents death. I hear a gunshot in the distance, and I am in town. No gunshots should be heard in the middle of the day while in town. I tell Ashley there were four car alarms going off in the parking lot at Walmart. All in a row. Warning signs of something coming in and then I found the dime representing Lances wounds and death.

I find I am amazed by the messages coming in to let me know of my childhood friend Lance is reaching out to me. Jesus is giving me signs of His presence and I now I start to see beyond the veil. Knowing the angles are calling out to me. As Jesus helps teach me it is all real.

My sister Vicky just moved into a trailer park near our hometown. Far from where she thought her heart was. Her and her husband just split up. Another failed marriage in our family of origin. My sister left an unhealthy relationship and uprooted herself again. My sister's daughter's Amber and Raina both have gifts of seership. They see, feel, hear, smell and know of the spirit around them. My nieces fear what is being presented to them. Their darkened world comes out and the negative energy creates several dark angels that surround them. Fear always is a mirror of what goes on within our heart and souls. We draw the light which we are creating in our reality. Raina and Amber struggle with the darkness in their lives, so the dark shadows vibrate into their lives.

In their trailer a small girl keeps appearing. A little girl in the spirit world, showing herself in Raina and Amber's reality. They see her with their naked eye. They are not sure who she is or what she wants. They just sense something dark coming in from her. Fear is present within both of my nieces and the darker spirits feed off that. They multiply.

I feel that a lot of children who suffer with nightmares and night terrors experience this very thing. Fear can induce many negative entities to vibrate into your realm of reality.

I ask Ashley for assistance with this case. My sister has asked me to assist her with ridding her home of the negative energy and the spirit that is haunting her girls. Raina and Amber can't sleep, and they walk around in fear in their own home because of the presence of this spirit.

In the night, one-night Raina explains there is a knife and it just lands between her feet.

Amber explains she hears whispers of her name all the time. While she tries to sleep, she hears;

"Amber, Amber, Amber".

Conversation with my sister Vicky, leads us to the following information as Ashley connects into the vibration of this energy/entity.

Ashley tells me 'this little girl' is around the age of eight or nine years old.

She has wavy brown hair. She holds a white lily flower at her shoulder. Ashley sees she has little brown freckles on her face.

She sees a bar stool and the little girl turns her back to Ashley. Ashley sees she has a long ponytail as she has turned around

Next…

Ashley sees she has a bright purple bouncy ball. A big one she bounces up and down the driveway.

After she takes Ashley to the driveway, the little girl leads Ashley to the rocks and water. Ashley sees there is a trailer there as well. The little girl shares with Ashely; 'this is my second visit'.

Ashley asks the little girl her name. "My name is Lily". Confirmation comes in for Ashley.

Ashely asks Lily; "are you the girl from the trailer"?

She says; "Yes I am". Ashley gets confirmation as she feels chills all up and down her body.

Lily has a ball in her hands. A large purple rubber ball. Lily runs up and down the driveway with this rubber ball. This little girl wants to play with her. The message is clear.

Ashley tells me; "she is lonely".

"She doesn't have anyone to play with her".

Ashley says; "I see her on a tire swing".

"she's down by the edge of the stream by the willow tree".

Ashley starts to cry. She feels the little girls lonely heart. As Lily swings on the tire swing, back and forth. It is dark and Ashley feels Lily's sadness.

Ashley keeps seeing the letter, 'R'.

Lily wants Ashley to go into the trailer with her.

As Ashely and I are in my home, this is what is coming through the veil to Ashley. We stand in the kitchen and Ashley experiences a connection with 'Lily' the little girl who is haunting my nieces at my sister's house. Ashley is picking up the energy and the messages through the conversation I have with my sister over the phone. Mediumship and being a seer, a skill that total astounds me, as I learn how to communicate with spirt/ghosts/ entities.

Lily wants Ashley to go to the trailer with her. Lily says; "There is something in the backyard, I want you to see".

There is water out back, a rock and a willow tree.

Ashley asks me; "is there a trailer in a town that starts with the letter, 'B'?" or 'D'. Lily keeps showing me these letters. I tell Ashley, "my sister lives in Brownville".

Ashley tells me; "She really wants me to see this". "I feel like I have drowned". "I think the letter 'D' is drowned."

"I feel like no one knew she was even gone." "She was just hanging by the stream and couldn't swim. There is one big rock that Ashley is seeing. I see a field with milk weeds and dandelions. "I see baby tennis shoes".

"Her mom is still alive". "Lily tells me she didn't know who her dad was".

Ashley has an overwhelming feeling she needs to find them. The little girls mom and dad.

As the information comes in Ashley googles the girl's name. Her name is Lily. From Brownville.

It's not the right girl or family.

The trailer was moved, and she is not where it is now.

My sister called to see who lived in this trailer before her. She received confirmation of this information. Lily's family's trailer was moved in 1999. The park was originally owned by a woman named Donna; she is in her 60's.

Research on who the little girl is and the information coming in lead to an old school friend of my sister's and me. The information led to Robin N's name and her family history.

Robin lived in the trailer before my sister started living in it. Robin lived in Brownville where my sister is living now. She died from cancer. She was a smoker and a drinker. She was drowning in sadness. Robin lived in Derby before this. There was an eight-year old girl. Her name was Jessica. There were 2 boys Douglas and Tony. Robin went to bed with her children one night and there was a house fire. Waking up the house ablaze Robin climbed out the window. In her efforts to go back into get her three children she got burnt. The firefighters pulled Robin out and her three children died that night.

Lynn N., Robin's sister was one of my best friends growing up. My friend Lance, Robin, Lynn my sister Vicky and my siblings and me, we knew each other and grew up together. The messages of the dime with the leaf shaped holes in them.

Heads up! A message is coming through. The year 1996 was found. The information came in on 10/26/15.

Vicky found a dime tail's up...

The year 2014 with deep scars on her dime. Robin died of cancer in the year 2014.

Robins mother's name was Marietta. She used to date our dad.

Ashley had another visit from Robin (Lily). The little girl representing as 'lily'. (Robin's inner-child lost).

Vicky calls me and we are talking like we do several times a week. Ryan, her son cries out from the bedroom, in agony. He is sitting on the bed and he is holding his foot rocking back and forth. My sister goes to him while we are talking on cellphones. Ryan is rolling around on the bed in pain. Vicky takes his hand away from his foot and it is twisted and distorted. It's like a he has a bad Charlie horse. It is an entity that has attached itself to my nephew's foot. It is twisting and hurting my nephew. It is more than just a Charlie horse. This experience lasts for over five minutes. While Ryan is crying out in pain.

Vicky and I stay calm while Ryan is in agony experiencing this entity attached to his foot.

After my communication with Ashley and 'Lily' then talking with my sister, the puzzle pieces started to fit together. Vicky asked me if I could help her. If I knew how to rid the spirit from the house. I told her I would be out in a few days to help if I could.

Making Peace with Robin

After three days of visits, dreams and signs Ashley and I end up on a long road trip to Brownville to my sisters trailer. Robin (Lily) will not leave or stop presenting herself in my sister's home.

More activity happens over the next few days. Vicky tells me she needs help.

Knives thrown at Raina's feet while she makes a midnight snack before bed and Amber keeps hearing her name being called in the night.

Messages: Willow tree, rocks, water, orange tree markers, and baby tennis shoes. These are just a few of the signs received by Ashley and me over the past few days before we head to my sisters to release Robin's spirit from her trailer.

We pray and center ourselves in the Christ Light. It is a long ride to Brownville from Stetson and Dexter. It is raining and dark. We listen to Paul Cardell's c.d. 'Miracles'. Music that I have been listening to since connecting to the spirit world.

The perfect song plays as I hear Robin, *"I want to go home to my children"*.

'The Memory Lives On', is the song playing when robin speaks to my heart.

I come to understand through my connection with Jesus that Robin's children are waiting for me to release Robin's spirt from this world into the next. A ritual that the Lord directs me to, through my Lakota Indian connection that I have been learning.

It is raining and very dark. It is hard to see driving. The closer we get to my sisters the harder it seems to be raining.

I call on Jesus Christ, Mother Mary, Saint Michael, Gray Eagle, Running Bull, White Calf Buffalo Woman and all the saints and angels. I call them in to lead Ashley and me, to protect us. I ask for clarity on what needs to be done to help Robin release from this world into the next. I want to assist Robin so her spirit can be at peace and she can be with her children.

Ashley and I arrive with flashlights and shovel. The clues lead us to a symbolic gravesite out back of my sister's trailer. There is a pine tree behind the trailer with several smaller rocks and one large rock. There is a willow tree with a tire swing down to the left of the trailer, near the stream. As we walk out towards the pine tree I see the orange markers on the ground, almost leading us to where Robin had described. It is raining hard and Ashley and I are soaked to the skin. There are three smaller rocks and one big rock. In between these rocks is an orange marker in the center. As if this spot was marked for a reason. Ashley and I dig. We start to wonder, what will we find. We continue to dig, and it seems like forever, for the rain is coming down hard and our adrenaline is running high. We are frightened of what we might find but we keep on taking turns digging. After a while we come to what appears to be a blue baby's blanket.

Under the freshly soaked soil is a decomposed baby's blanket. Ashley and I had dug until we found what Robin had told us was buried there after her children had died. It was her baby boy, Tony's blanket.

We stop and cry and hug one another. Ashley and I understand the significance with what we just found. We have found a precious gravesite that Robin had dug and buried her little boys blanket. As Ashley and I go into my sisters trailer we share with her what we found. My sister, Amber, Raina and Ryan are scared to death. We all join hands in the living room. We say a prayer together. I have lite candles all around the living room and kitchen. I do this to bring in the Light of God. To dispel the negative energy. I open a window to let the spirit in the house be released.

I do a house clearing after we stand in a circle in the living room to send up the intention and prayer to release Robin's spirit and her heart up to her children.

I sage my sister's house with white sage, I burn it and use a smudge fan to cleanse the house. I use a smudge fan to disperse the smoke in all corners and around all doors and windows, sending up a prayer for no evil spirit to enter.

We released Robin from her pain and tears. We found her little gravesite out back of my sisters trailer. We have released Robins spirit to the heavens above. We have helped assist her to transition from this world into the next. A painful knowing that Robin's pain kept her spirit heavily burdened and she could not move on.

Jesus assisted me to help Robin join with her babies in heaven. The spiritual warfare is true and very painful to understand. After this experience I completely understand the darkness in this world.

After an exhausting spiritually heightened few days we thought we had done well. Little did we know there was one more piece!

As Ashely and I conversed with Vicky and the girls and my nephew Ryan, we explained what we saw and found out back. We explained about the signs and symbols we received to come to this point in our assisting Robin to move on to be with her children.

I mention to Vicky about the willow tree, the tire swing, the rocks, and the orange markers. We tell my sister about the baby's tennis shoes.

The only clue we hadn't found. Where did the tennis shoes fit in. As I mentioned this to my sister she went to her bedroom were Ryan was experiencing the attachment of Robin. Vicky pulls out of her jewelry box a pair of white baby tennis shoes. A pair she had for her first son. When I saw the shoes, I got large all over goose bumps. Confirmation of all the communication and what just transpired.

The tennis shoes revealed to me that at some point in the short period that my sister had moved in with her family that Robin had attached herself to Ryan, Vicky's youngest son. When Ryan had the twisted foot and ankle that was Robin's way of showing Vicky the pain that her baby's had suffered in the fire and her own pain that she couldn't save her children from the fire. The agony that Robin must have suffered and losing her children in the fire was only part of her sad story. Robin got cancer and spent the last days in agony and suffering over the loss of her children. Robin was unable to move on because of her broken spirit. She was heavy hearted and didn't know what to believe. She had lost her faith in God. Robin was wandering aimlessly until she found Ryan to attach to.

After this discovery of the baby tennis shoes and the explanation of all that transpired Ryan ran crying to the bathroom. Ryan in fear and not fully understanding what just transpired thought that he was going to die. He Thought that Robin was going to kill him. The spiritual attack on my nephew is something that I have found out, is a true experience that some people are being subjected to.

All by the power of Jesus Christ have I learned this truth of His spiritual warfare.

"Believe it or leave it". A message from Jesus Christ.

10/29/15

Miracles- Paul Cardell- his song plays in my head all night long.

I dream of one single angle worm, long and tall. It burrows in the soil.

I get the word; *"slugger".*

"You are a real trooper".

"The Scooby Doo Crew". A message from the angels and 'Miss Felicia'.

"I will know what I know when I know it." "Not one second beforehand"

CHAPTER 5

His Captive Heart

Poetry in E-Motion

In the first of my communication with Jesus Christ I was going through a whirlwind of emotions and feeling the veil being removed was very unsettling. As a budding artist erupts from my hands, I was writing my experiences at the speed of light. The information from God was coming in fast. I was having downloads into my unconscious mind. A plethora of information was flooding my sense day and night. I was having backlogged information flow into my conscious mind. The Lord shows me this morning some of the beauty within the writings. I found to be flowing into my consciousness. He asks me to place some of our writings here.

It feels like poetry and it has true tones of music within the full sentences. Automatic writing as I try to figure out what it is God needs from me. I have come to learn I love to write. I love the messages and knowing that I do not sit alone or walk alone. The Lord forever and always guides my hands if I listen to my heart.

Little books erupt and this one titled: *His Holy Grail- The Missing Links;* connects me back to the thoughts of *'DaVinci Code'* and the underlying drama and suspense in the knowing of things that are beyond the human mind. History and legend meeting in the movie that Dan Brown so beautifully portrayed and Tom Hanks starred in.

His Captive Heart

The missing Sanskrit's. Tablets written and lost. Tablets destroyed.
I am still given puzzle pieces and I know not what the end results
will be. Mysteries revealed to me and empty pieces of my heart
unfolds one breath at a time, and I feel lost and all alone.

Prophecy revealed to a lonely child of God and she tries to save the world
from a chair. Chained to His heart and unable to breathe on her own.
Silence for far too long and He needs parts of His mysteries revealed and
she feeds her own soul one hour at a time and one lost soul at a time.

It starts with a special child. A missing child from Maine and turns into a whirlwind gone from bad to unimaginable. Messages from the other side from a lonely child in pain and sorrow for a world quickly drowning in a sea of their own blood shed.

Consciously unaware of this eminent fate, over ten years ago and she was locked up in a prison of her own. Searching and reaching out from a body that turns out to be that of someone else's.

Blueprints revealed to her and she has no idea where to turn but to Him, to Jesus Christ.

He tries to teach her so many great mysteries and her own reality is taken from her three times. Jesus comes back time and time again and has faith in her abilities to get this special project where it needs to be.

Messages of seals broken, hearts bleeding blue blood. Tears of blue flow from her own eyes as He cries His own tears through her own body. A painful journey for all three. The Father, Son and Mother. Jesus tells me He is sorry for all His love lost. A love He shares with her has been from before the beginning of time.

We all pay a high price for our own choices and He tries to teach us, and we fail to sit and listen to our inner-selves. The inner voice that cries out to be heard. It is His voice. The Lord's voice.

We question daily why we are here. Where are we from? Failing or succeeding in all we do is solely in our hands based on the choices He plants in our brains.

She struggles daily to follow His breath. He breathes within her heart and she fails and falls. She picks herself up after she fails Him. Time and time again. Patience is a great valued attribute and she works tirelessly to find the values that were not given to her as a natural source due to lost souls of her own parents.

Another book Jesus Christ asks me to write and I have no idea
where it will lead me on this journey. He pushes me daily;
onward. I love Him that much and my heart belongs to Jesus
Christ. I ask questions and I fear only failing Him.

Mindfulness and meditation are of utmost importance for His journey
with me to be successful. Connecting to my center. My heart is His
Lion Heart. Pure and white it roars words, phrases and pictures run past
my third eye. I see things beyond the veil. I hear His voice from within
my own heart. Our hearts are connected as one. It's beat can be felt
inside of my own. An exhilarating feeling and a love felt like no other.

Only time will tell what these next pages unfold. I hold my breath
and hope for His love to shine through all the words He helps
me put to paper for special eyes to see His love come forth.

Is it a waste of time? I hope not for your world,
my world and His world depends on it.

Jesus Christ reveals to me He is dying from the inside out. One breath
at a time. He shows me His own breath taken away as each day passes.
I feel it within my own lungs. I am not sure how much more I can take.
He tells me; "You are your mother's daughter". "You are my own strength".

Jesus gives me my wings in a dream. A vision. An amazing gift. He
now allows me to feel those wings. They grow and become stronger
every day. I only wonder if they will carry me away before I am able
to reach those who He asks me to reach before it is too late?

The world is upside down and Jesus has come in flesh form, to
rectify all the choices that have been made. Who, what, when,
where, and why? Questions only He knows. I am all that I am,
because of the One who sent me. I am a vessel of His Love and a
faithful servant of the Lord; I am a Captive of His Heart...

Poetry is Emotion in its rarest form…

Poetry written as I hold a special angel's hand. She steps forward a month before I go to speak publicly for the first time in a long time. I walk through all the doors the Lord sees will help others. I will be lecturing on the importance of journaling and writing your story or your families story. The legend and legacy of our own family. Record keepers help keep God's love stories alive. I encourage others to heal themselves through writing. A gift I learn as a teenager. I will be speaking at a drug rehabilitation center. Mental illness is running rampant and drug abuse is at an all-time high. A special group I will speak in front of and I hope to touch some of their hearts and help give them hope. Drug addicts and mentally unstable children of God. I hope to give them purpose and a reason to stay here. I hope to see a spark, or a fire ignited in their own hearts, as I share my own story of survival. I hope to share how I overcame my own fears. I hope to share love and even the light that saved me can be seen by them. I hope to share they too can be their own hero.

Amber Jade steps forward from the spirit world. I see the signs before me. I see, '*Opioids*' and I see the football. I see her son and her daughter presented to me several times this week. I see a little girl in need of her mother. One she will never know of; for Ambers struggles and addition led to an early death. She leaves behind a young boy trying to find his own way. His grandmother ends up being the rock for this young boy and his younger sister. They both lean on their grandmother through it all. Amber asks me to share a piece of her story. I do it in poetry form as she knows I will be speaking to those in need just like she was before she drowned in her own pain and sorrows. I hope to honor you honey, and I hope this will help your heart to know these special souls have a connection to you and now I do too. They are never to be forgotten. The Lord holds them all even if they do not realize it.

Be Your Own Hero...

A message from A.J., mother, daughter, granddaughter and sister. Not just an addict that lost her battle. She suffered with diabetes and its complications took a toll on her body. Just a few months after she gave birth to her little girl the Lord took her home to be with Him.

"Life's Struggle"

I lost my battle and now I see all the pain my struggles left behind
My mom carries the burden of it all
I struggled with fear and it got me up here
I couldn't fight the demons in my head anymore
I had no clue. I had not self-worth
Seeing life from the other side is so painful
My choices and my fear of self-love got me down
I tried so hard to find the one
That perfect love
A man I just had to have
A man to make me complete
The best part of me I had to leave behind

My son and daughter

They are the best part of me

I lost and so did they

My addiction and my health

My body and my mind it let me down

I struggled with diabetes most of my childhood

Always seeing others living it up eating whatever they wanted

Having all they wanted

It broke my heart

Jealousy is always the devil in disguise

My son and daughter live on without me and I see all they do

It's painful to watch them from the other side

I miss out on so much love from them. Yet, I see mom

Does such great job

I never learned to appreciate all her hard work

Her love, I see now was all her nagging

Even the heavy hand that hurt so bad

Her own fears and frustration coming out with a whack or two on my behind

I see her life was more difficult than my own

Explanations from God of why my mother never gave up on me

Why my own mother always tried so hard

Football games, poolside days remembered

We always were surrounded by people, fun and laughter

Always the wrong crowd I could find it every time

Stepping out of this world allows me to see

The mistakes I made that made me want to leave

My last days were so painful

I drowned in my own sorrows

Something I can never be a part of

All their tomorrows

I see my kids pain I see them cry tears

They miss me, but I wish they knew I will always be near
My heart is part of their own and I will always feel them
My heart and my soul lives within them
I wish nothing but the best for my babies
I can't wait to hold them once again
I will always be flying around like a little pestering honeybee
Sucking up all the sweet love I see from the other side
My eyes never leave them, I peek in on them all day
long Buzzing and whispering in their ears all the time…

A.J. a mother that lost her battle with mental illness
and drug addiction. Her message!!

BE YOUR OWN HERO!!!

Footsteps of Christ

I hear His light steps just behind me on the pavement
I hear the gentle rhythm of Christ's footsteps
He has been on my heels the whole way
Pushing me on this journey into His Light
Pulling me back from the flames
Life's challenges everyday
Each time I fall I hear His footsteps quicken
I go left; He follows
I go right; He follows
I fall down Christ is there to pick me up
He follows me all the days of my life
His breath I hear whisper in my ear
"Slow down, my darling"
I learn to call on Him the heavier my cross becomes
Falling to my knees I find Him
Then up again I go; His footsteps just behind me
Running through this world; with His footsteps always
Just behind me
One fall day; He wakes me gently
In the night, our dreams coming home
Our dreams become one
And Christ's footsteps no longer behind me
For His footsteps are my own
He carries me home
Driving my very soul everyday
He teaches me to slow the pace; He teaches me to pray
He teaches me all I ever knew
Jesus Christ holds me up; His loving arms, I am
I no longer hear His footsteps follow me
For Christ carries me through it all….

A poem I write as I find my way home!!

CHAPTER 6

Dreams, Visions and Experiences in the year 2021

Bella Louise Allen

January 30, 2021

It's hard to imagine another year has come and gone. So many books and too many lessons and loses over the years to count. I open another book for the Lord. In June of 2015 I started writing my own story. A sad recount of my own life. One Our Father and Christ, Jesus tells me has touched their very souls. I wonder this morning how many other stories have touched the creator's heart and soul. As I learn of more history, the Father and His Son bring it forward, I learn they have seen it all and experienced it all with us.

Who understands the *"Holy Spirit of God"* like I have been taught? I am not sure.

I record all that I am taught in hopes of someday enlightening those that are scholars, theologians and learned Elders. Those who have been highly respected and thought better of for the education that they have paid a high price for. I continue to hope that the Catholic Church will take notice of the books I have written and sent them since August of 2016. Books portraying God's broken Sacred Heart, for the children of the world.

The Lord tells me; *"no one has paid a higher price for their education than you have"*.

So many similarities in our stories, the Lord and me.

Being born into poverty and a family with much love. I feel blessed to be alive and God knows, somedays I wish I could bring Him down in *"flesh form"*. He reminds me; *"I have only walked as closely with one woman as I do with you"*.

"That was the woman who bore me into this world".

We start another book and I am asked by Christ; *"never lose hope"*. *"For Father would surely die if you did"*.

I am asked to walk on with my head held high and to record the lessons He brings forward. I am asked to never give up for it surely would break His heart. I do all that I do for the Passion of Christ!!!

8:00 a.m.

January 30, 2021

This is the day in between my eldest son's birth and my daughter's birth. As I sit and ponder the dream in the early morning hours, the Lord asks me to start another book. Three-hundred and forty pages in the thirty-second book I have written since June of 2015. God reminds me; *"That is a miracle in itself"*.

The Lord revisits more of our story in the night. He brings forward a man I miss greatly. A faithful Catholic man and he was a veteran of the United States of America. What branch he served in; I do not remember? So many tales Larry and I shared together. A special man to be remembered and God reminds me to look back through our books, all thirty-two of them. He reminds me of the history of our country and our world. God reminds me of His Love Story from the beginning of time as we understand it as humans.

History recorded in books of all kinds are set before me when Jesus Christ and Our Father teach me. Books I struggled to learn from when I was a child. My life was filled with such drama and trauma I could hardly focus on each moment back in those days, let alone learn history or science. It just wouldn't sink in. Dates and names of history from way back. I always received low grades. Just barely getting by in school because of the trauma's in my life I could never concentrate.

God sees the needs of His children. Something that is an ongoing theme in the books I write for Our Father. Jesus Christ has come to life within me and His Passion is revisited daily with me. I recite the *"Our Father, the Hail Mary, and Divine Mercy Chaplet"*, prayers in the night before I fall asleep. Something that warms the Trinities Heart. Calming the mind and connecting back to God's very heart is what I have learned I do when I pray. I also have learned it soothes the Father's Soul to know we need Him. As I lay in the fetal position and recite these prayers, I feel Christ's closeness.

I feel my Heavenly Mother's closeness. I feel the Creator's closeness. I feel such love it can't be described.

A couple of dreams in the night and I recognize the Archangels present themselves as a huge pastel colored butterfly in my dream. The angels can present themselves any way they wish. Last night however, I see them as a multi-colored, pale yellow, pink, purple, orange, green and blue striped butterfly. I see the wings and they seem to be made of embroidery thread. Their wings are crocheted, as if a grandmother had made this butterfly. I try frantically in my dream to catch a picture of this amazingly beautiful butterfly. I try to open the screen of my cellphone and it will not open. My heart panics and I want so desperately to capture a memory or proof of this phenomenon that floats, flutters and flies before my eyes in my dream.

I see the Lord has taken me home. In my dream I see a large brown bear. He wanders all around the homestead at the place where I grew up. He looks all around and sees it all. Every painful moment I have lived. Every playful moment I have ever enjoyed. Every tear I have cried, I see *"Papa Bear"*, God; Our Father has seen it all….

I see the extended porch again, on the front of our little humble home. A meaning of God has saved my very life. He extended my life, by giving me a second chance. He has created a miracle and wants it recognized.

I see the sewer has come up out of the ground all around our little house. I smell the stench of it; and I feel it between my toes as I walk barefoot on our front lawn. I try frantically to catch a glimpse of the beautiful butterfly. I want to capture a picture of this multi-colored butterfly on my phone.

I feel this part of the dream, God sees even though my life has been a complete mess, I have never let anything hold me back from loving. I feel even though sticky situations come into my life; I still see the beauty of everything God puts into my life.

Music, laughter and love always outshines the 'crappy' things that try to hold me back from being all God has hoped I would be.

In my dreamtime God takes me to Larry and Lorna's last home. God revisits a special couple I came to know when I ran Busy Bee's Cleaning Company. One of the many gifts God gave me was the ability to do most anything I set my mind to. Running my own business for twenty years and it helped sustain my needs and helped provide for my family and me for a long time.

I have met many people over the years. Through my nursing career and through the many business' I have run.

I ran a photography business for a short while. I ran a Reiki Studio briefly in the professional building in town. After COVID-19 I had to close the doors and then I moved. Now I run that business out of my apartment. I ran a cleaning company for twenty years and I even wanted to have my own catering business. I went to college for cooking because I wanted to have my own catering business. Something that would have taken a lot of startup money. That dream never came to fruition.

I always found myself coming back to nursing and caring for the elderly and those who had mental or physical ailments. I know my heart has always been with those less fortunate than myself. Always wanting to help others has been a passion I didn't understand.

In my dream in the night God takes me to Larry and Lorna's little place. They moved in the late stages of their own lives to live with their son and daughter-in-law.

Larry's daughter Marie had taken care of her mother and father for a lengthy time and passed on this job to her brother so she could have a semblance of a normal life before she wore herself out.

I see in this dream God shows me Larry and Lorna have passed on. I see the empty room that once held these two special souls. I feel my heart saddened for what God shows me.

Something I wish I could have done was talk to and connect one more time with Larry and Lorna. They always loved to ask me questions about my walk with Jesus Christ. Larry always was curious about personal things he knew I had found out about the Lord, that he felt no one else knew. I remember the day he told me; "I have never known anyone that has walked so close with the Lord, as you do".

I never thought too much about it, for it is our choice, isn't it? How close we allow the Lord to walk with us?

The Lord smiles at me, this morning as He reminds me of the question's Larry used to ask me. Larry asked me once "what is Jesus' favorite food?

I told him, right out of the blue, "Bacon". "God loves bacon".

Larry tells me, that's odd. "I thought Jews didn't eat meat"?

I told Larry; "I can only tell you that because He continually asks me to get bacon and have it with eggs, muffins and coffee with my sister".

So, I feel the Lord, loves eating bacon!

The Lord lays with me after He shows me that Larry and I spent some special moments hashing over our writings. Larry was the first man to read my book, "*The Tree of Knowledge is Mary's Sweet Vine*".

Larry shared with me it was the first book he had read in over fifty years. I felt honored to have him take the time to read my book. I felt him to be a very well educated and faithful man. A loving father and husband. I saw what might have been a glimpse of Our Father within him.

After reading my book, I asked Larry, "so what did you think"?

He smiled and I could see his wheels turning. I saw he was trying to think of an easy way of saying the next words that came out of his mouth.

Larry said, "I'm not sure if you're an angel or if you're the devil"!

As my heart began to hurt, I let that go right away. I saw God was testing me.

God knows I look for acceptance with all that I do and those words I felt briefly were a test. I felt the pain hit my heart, yet God let me release it right away.

The next thing Larry said, "I will be curious to see where these books take you".

He also asked me; "If you could see yourself in five years, where do you see yourself"?

I could not answer Larry, for I know I must let God take me and lead me every day.

A hard lesson came through in my dreamtime. To know God is more than likely showing me Lorna who suffered from Parkinson's Disease, just like my dad and Pope John Paul II; that she has more than likely died. A hard lesson to know, God is more than likely showing me that Larry has passed as well. It's been two years since I last saw either one of them. Larry's heart condition more than likely took him before Lorna's struggle with Parkinson's.

So many people have touched my life. So many lives I have aided and assisted in their own needs walking home to God.

God reminds me, *"I have seen it all". "I have seen all those who you took care of, for I am within them".*

Another dream enlightening my painful knowing.

10:00 a.m.

January 30, 2021

I bath in the Light of God daily. He illuminates all things for me today and I am asked to record all He sees I go through and all I continue to experience. I enlighten God's own truths. His reality.

Spiritual Warfare is real, and it takes a toll on God's Heart and His very Soul.

I hear many phrases, songs, Bible verses, dictionary words and names. They come through the veil. They come in on the winds of change.

The Truth of God is being revealed within this world and I wonder who is awakened to His painful heart?

I continue to hear the name; *"Matthew"* brought in through the winds. I hear it dropped into my consciousness. I keep being reminded of my nephew Matthew. A special boy the Lord sees and knows is struggling.

I am given the phrase; *"you can lead a horse to water, but you cannot make him drink"*.

A phrase with a powerful meaning as God shows me all He is up against today.

As the Trinity holds me up; I see Saint Michael this morning. He is my great protector. I come out around from the shield of God, and then there stands Saint Michael. I am reminded of the two swords I was shown a few days ago. I did not record seeing these swords, yet Saint Michael has me draw them and He reminds me of his great battle against the devil. Against Satan. The Spiritual Warfare God is up against.

I see one large sword. It rests between Heaven and Earth. It comes in straight down. I see the handle of this sword is made of gold. I see this golden handle that has scrolls on it. I see in the center of this golden handled sword, a single droplet of blood. From this single droplet of blood. I see it and it runs down to the tip of the sword, a deep red flow of blood.

Right after the vision of the sword with one single drop of blood, I am shown a huge sword. I see what looks like a small dagger. The view of this sword was shown to me in 3-D. If you look at it at an angle, it looked like a dagger. Yet I believe it was a sword. Depending on which angle you look at it. If you look straight on, it could have been a large sword. From the side it however, looked like a short dagger. I see the golden handle on this sword. I see the hand that holds it and I come to understand that hand is Our Father's. He holds the sword and it goes to the left angle. I see the sword's blade is made of crystal quartz. (Time). I see the sunshine, off this sword and I see the rays going from left to right. From side to side and from all angles of this beautiful sword. The Father reveals to me history as He shows me this sword going to the left, back through time.

Spiritual Warfare

An invisible enemy of God's. One I am familiar with.

I come to see the evil one. The devil, Satan. I see this spiritual warfare come down to the earth, through God's own children. Those who are sleeping and walking in this world creating hate and warfare. Those killing needlessly. Those drowning in the darkness.

My nephew Matthew has been the strength and fortress for many people in his life. His own mother was the first woman he loved. He supported and helped teach her many lessons over the years. He helped raise his own siblings as so many of God's children do. Baby's taking care of baby's and never having time to be a child themselves.

My nephew has been through a lot in his life. At the age of two I remember he climbs a ladder, just like Jesus did. To see a higher perspective of God's world; maybe! Just a memory brought forward as I write of the fear my sister experienced as my nephew ran back and forth on the roof of my godmother's trailer one day.

A ladder left out and if it had been taken care of this fear never would have been experienced. Matthew would never have gotten up on the roof and he would never have scared the daylights out of his mother.

A hidden message in this lesson. Always hidden message come with all I write. Shutting the Lord out and it's a message of; we continue to shut out God's light when we shut Jesus Christ out of our lives.

My nephew has been gifted with perseverance and fortitude. He has been gifted in seeing things from all sides of every situation. He has been gifted with a big heart. Something I am so familiar with. Matthew takes on the responsibility of my mother again, after I was kicked out. My mother took a fall off her front steps over a year ago and broke her shoulder. I moved in with her and she didn't like the changes that took place. I was trying to help my mother and her ego, fear and dementia got the best of the both of us. I had to leave my mom, for she was in such a state of mental unrest. She kicked me out of her home after I gave up my life to assist her.

I converse with my sister Vicky via text messaging yesterday. My sister has been having trouble sleeping and she has been experiencing many of the same things I have. Angels speaking out and reaching out through the veil.

Vicky's granddaughter, Vanessa has been calling out to my sister. Vanessa was Matthews first daughter. She died the night before her scheduled c-section. A perfect angel died from strep- B, a diagnosis missed and could have been prevented had the doctors caught it in time. A very painful experience for Matthew and his first wife. A situation that put them both in emotional turmoil that ruined their mental stability as a couple and eventually caused them to separate and divorce.

My own father and Vanessa (both who have crossed over) have been calling out and reaching out to me. To know the angel's, see and know of Matthews struggles is the lesson of the day.

Matthew is grieving and still not fully healed from his wife, Tracy leaving him. Tracy is my nephews second wife. A woman I have assisted with her own inner demons. She is a woman I helped release a negative entity from her being and conscious mind. Matthew is still not healed from the traumatic first marriage he had. He is still not healed from the loss of Vanessa. My nephew is struggling with the loss of his second marriage, one he didn't want to end.

Matthew struggles with anger, loss, addiction and he carries a huge burden as he tries to care for his grandmother and all her needs.

His two children live most of the time with their mother. Matthews ex-wife is a wounded soul and her past comes spilling out in all the decisions she makes. Whether they are right or wrong, I am not judging, just understanding her emotional state affects the very lives of her children.

As Matthew tries to live a semblance of a normal life. I come to understand he is struggling.

Mom tells me he is drinking. He is taking pain medication to help him with his broken ankle. Something that happened in amongst all the chaos that was already going on in his life. A warning sign from God, is what I understand that to be. He slows us down when we need it most and then we get up and keep on going without looking at the underlying issues.

As Matthew struggles with alcohol and over medicating himself, I come to understand my father and Vanessa are witnessing Matthews pain. I come to understand the Lord sees and feels his pain. I come to understand the angels try to get me and my sister Vicky to understand he needs help.

Hence, the phrase; *"you can lead a horse to water, but you cannot make him drink"*.

Always a double meaning. This phrase brings forward an underlying issue. My nephew is drinking his pain away. He is medicating his pain away.

As I converse with Vicky yesterday; she shares with me her son stated to her; "if it wasn't for the kids, I would kill myself". A bold statement and a fear impending statement in these emotional times today.

"I wouldn't do that to them". He states afterward.

From my own experience I come to understand we hide behind a mask. We hide behind work. We hide behind food. We hide behind alcohol and drugs. We lose our very soul and being and the purpose why we came, when we do not stand up to the issues underlying the cause of our actions. We drown our pain in 'things'.

Jesus Christ has become my own counselor. He helps me daily come to grips with my past, present and even future struggles. He holds my hand and revisits past traumas with me and asks me; "How are you feeling about this today"?

God will show me a past traumatic event and sometimes I know we must discuss or go over the feelings it brought up within me. Sometimes I cry about the lessons He brings forward and then He wipes away my tears and I move on.

A great gift the Lord shares with me.

Knowing in the Bible, He states "I will wipe away every tear".

Revelation 21:4- *"And God shall wipe away all tears from their eyes; and there shall be no more death, neither sorrow, nor crying, neither shall there be any more pain; for the former things are passed away".*

I come to see the angels, God the Father and Jesus Christ share with me my own nephew's pain. My sister and I discuss the reality of her world, and knowing the angels are reaching out to her in her sleep and during the day. Warnings and premonitions of the sad world we live in. The reality of my nephew and his life as Vicky and I try to work and live our own lives. Being awakened and an empath can be so very overwhelming. Sad knowing as this entry enlightens my reality since 2006.

The knowing is not all it's cracked up to be. To see beyond the veil. To know other's pain. To feel my nephew's pain and sorrow and not be able to help him. To know only God can help him in these dark times.

My sister Vicky and I have always been close. As I converse and learn, she is struggling with her son, and her two daughters. The lost generation continues to figure it all out without Jesus to help lead or support them. I come to understand the angels are bringing Vicky the knowledge of her son, Matthews struggles.

Vicky is going to have a stress test done because she is not sleeping, and she is having anxiety and chest pains. Something I can sympathize with, yet I cannot get her to understand her empathy for her children and her underlying painful heart, may very well be God showing her He understands her painful heart for her children.

I told my sister, I would never know, now if I had an underlying heart condition, for I feel such pain from the knowing of God's own broken heart. I feel the arrows pierce my heart every day now.

I know God calls out to us all. He calls from the wilderness for us all to love ourselves. For, who else could love us the way we deserve. Jesus knocks on all our hearts. He calls out to us. He calls out to us, to let Him in so He can teach us of His great love.

I am taught by the Lord; He is the only one who could love us and teach us all these lessons. I sit and contemplate. I pray and I learn copious amounts of hard lessons from the Lord daily.

Grateful to be alive.

Grateful to be awakened by the Lord. Grateful He holds me so tight.

I pray for my nephew. I pray Matthew will draw upon the Lord's strength for it would certainly change the fate of his own children's lives if they lost their father to alcohol, drugs or even if he decided to end his precious life.

Real life and real struggles I share for I do know God's pain through all that I am. Through all those that I love. Family is our greatest gift.

Christ was our greatest gift from the Creator. I just wish I could share with others His beauty and love for each of us....

9:15 a.m.

January 31, 2021

Thirty-one years ago; today, I gave birth to my first-born child in this lifetime.

A reality many do not understand. The past, present and future of all God's children. The Holy Spirit understood. The angels understood. Generations of God's soul's and spirit's understood.

My daughter is on a journey, just like I have been. Wandering around in this deep dark valley trying to figure out what her path and plan is.

What are God's plans for her? Where does she fit in? What is she here to accomplish? In the night I have a visit from the *'dark side'*.

I see the Angel of death. I see Archangel Azrael in my dreamtime and always and forever I am taught deep lessons in God's reality and in His fight for life.

I am taken to the home that I was first aware of that was *'home'* to me. I was just an infant child and we lived in poverty and what appears by the photos, as squalor. I'm not even sure what that word means, yet it seems appropriate for the sentence. I have learned many dictionary words over the course of this journey. Words handed to me by the angels. Lessons brought forward by God's Holy Angels and the spirit that surround and love to teach me.

In the night I see what appears to be *'Satan'*. I come to understand the angels can and will teach me all that God needs me to know. I believe Saint Azrael appears in this dream to teach me this lesson.

I am taken back to the first property that my mother and father had while I was an infant. I see the tiny old worn boards on the little house. I see the large cracks that separated these boards yet kept a family of seven within its walls.

I see outside this worn house an old vehicle held up on blocks. I see it is freshly painted. Pure white is the color this car has been repainted. The wet paint runs down the front of this old car and I see God is showing me my *'new'* vessel or vehicle. My new body.

I come to understand the Lord repurposes some of His old souls. A message given to Saint Bernadette when Mother Mary appeared to her. *"I will not make you happy in this world, but the next".* A meaning I hold close to my own heart.

I am taught by a beautiful saint, *'One out of every three stars falls back down to earth'.* These two quotes and messages touch base on a huge part of this lesson today.

Prophecy: *"**And the stars shall fall from heaven**".* Matthew 24:29 Reincarnation and Incarnate souls.

I am reminded as I write of the phrase; *"She has an old soul"*!

The Lord reminds me, *"you look pretty good for a dead woman"*!

All conversations and lessons I have been taught and contemplated with the Lord and His Holy Angel's.

The dream in the night and I feel the presence of my entire spirit family. Ones from this incarnation. I see a large pond filled with water in the center of the yard. I see God is referencing the tears cried over the generations with our family. One family from His Tree of Life.

As I try to go back in time with my lessons in love the Lord shows me the future all His children are faced with. In this dream I see a darkened world. Worse than what we see and know of today.

I see there are large pits and holes all over the lawn at my old homestead. Some have more water pooled within these holes. Others not so many. Painful memories and then some not as painful.

As I try to go home, to my mother's house, which just happens to be one mile south of the first home I remember, I see the darkness before me. I try to go home to my mother and the trees are all uprooted and falling into the road.

I see the different levels of the road as it heaves and moves with the frost in the ground thawing. I turn back for the trees I see are so thick and hindering on my journey, I just give up and go back.

I see my own children in this dream. I see they struggle and try their best to do all that they are trying to do. I see my son Paul. He is trying to clean out the septic system and it just keeps pumping old feces out onto the lawn.

I decide to go the long way around to get to my mother's house and as I do, I run into the devil. I see Satan and the darkness, just seems to get worse. I see large chunks of earth and it is muddy and soupy and the different layers of this ground is uneven and very frightful, not knowing where to place my feet. I see almost down into the depths of hell. To the left of Satan, I see a large firepit. He stokes it up and grins as he sees I struggle to find my way out of this living hell in my dream.

I wake to a pounding chest on the couch at work. I wake with an ache in the pit of my stomach. I wake with the knowing God's children have a long hard road ahead of them without Jesus Christ or the love of His Mother to guide them.

This dream I feel was triggered by the fact that my grandson who is six years old has been dealing with and experiencing nightmares. He has been reaping what he sows in the daytime hours I find out yesterday as my daughter posts, 'Curtis has won a game'. 'He has defeated the devil'. A video game he has been playing for a while now and he defeated and went through all the levels of the game and at the end of the game, he pissed on the devil. (I can only imagine the pictures and graphics that are running through his tiny little brain).

I feel part of this dream is a bleed through of what Curtis may be experiencing through his own dreams. I understand God brings to my consciousness the connection with my grandson's dreamtime. I see the darkness that he is experiencing. I come to understand, the more you deal in the darkness, the more darkness will come into your life.

A hard lesson to learn for so many.

The Lord helps me to understand why Curtis is having his nightmares. The *'game'* he plays is becoming his reality in his unconscious mind. A reality for so many of God's children. A deep lesson for me, as I wish I could get my daughter and grandson to understand, you play in the darkness that is what you will get....

History: *Stars fall from heaven*

In 1833, the last of the signs appeared which were promised by the Savior as tokens of his second advent. Said Jesus, *"The stars shall fall from heaven."* Matt: 24:29.

And John in the Revelation declared, as he beheld in a vision the scenes that herald The Day of God: *"The stars of heaven fell unto the earth, even as a fig-tree casteth her untimely figs, when she is shaken of a mighty wind."* Rev. 6:13.

This prophecy received a striking and impressive fulfillment in the great meteoric shower of November 13, 1833. That was the most extensive and wonderful display of falling stars which has ever been recorded; "The whole firmament, over all the United States, being then, for hours, in fiery commotion".

No celestial phenomenon has ever occurred in this country, since its first settlement, which was viewed with such intense admiration by one class in the community, or such dread and alarm by another." "it's sublimity and awful beauty still linger in many minds... Never did rain fall much thicker than the meteors fell toward the earth; east, west, north and south, it was the same. In a word, the whole heavens seemed in motion....The display, as described in Professor Sillman's journal, was seen all over North America... From two o'clock until broad daylight, the sky being perfectly serene and cloudless, an incessant play of dazzlingly brilliant luminosities was kept up in the whole heavens."

"No language indeed can come up to the splendor of the magnificent display; no one who did not witness it can form an adequate conception of its glory. It seemed as if the whole starry heavens had congregated at one point near the zenith, and were simultaneously shooting forth, with the velocity of lightning, to every part of the horizon; and yet they were not exhausted— thousands swiftly followed in the track of thousands, as if created for the occasion." A more correct picture of a fig-tree casting its figs when blown by a mighty wind, it is not possible to behold."

On the following day its appearance, Henry Dana Ward wrote thus of the wonderful phenomenon: "No philosopher or scholar has told or recorded an event, I suppose, like that of yesterday morning. A prophet eighteen hundred years ago foretold it exactly, if we will be at the trouble of understanding stars falling to mean falling stars, in the only sense in which it is possible to be literally true."

Thus, was displayed the last of those signs of his coming, concerning which Jesus bade his disciples, *"When ye shall see all these things, know that it is near, even at the doors."* Matt 24:33. After these signs, John beheld, as the great event next impending, the heavens departing as a scroll, while the earth quaked, mountains and islands removed out of their places, and the wicked in terror sought to flee from the presence of the Son of man.

Many who witnessed the falling of the stars, looked upon it as a herald of the coming Judgement, --"*an awful type, a sure forerunner, a merciful sign, of that great and dreadful day."* Thus, the attention of the people was directed to the fulfillment of prophecy, and many were led to give heed to the warning of the second advent....

Message: The Lord brings forward all lessons and as I record this for Our Father. He holds me tight. *"No more fear"*...

"Only LOVE"!!!

Bella Louise Allen

7:28 a.m.

February 1, 2021

A long thirty-six-hour shift over soon. I am nudged before the end of my shift to record yesterday's song of the day.

I see, hear and feel Pope John Paul II, John Bosco and Padre Pio. They sing in unison as I stand in the kitchen. Always and forever the Trinity shows me itself, in threes. Never a more beautiful reminder of this yesterday afternoon of their love for me.

John Paul II tells me; *"This is my finest work, since my death"*. He references the love story he helps me write. The lesson the other day in my dreamtime, was the Father's doing, yet I am shown John Paul II lecturing me and teaching me, history, and English, poetry and reminding me the importance of music and a playful heart. I see in another dream, me sitting as a student with John Paul II teaching me at the head of the classroom.

Later in the day.

As I stand in the kitchen I hear *"How do you solve a problem like Maria?"*

Saint Padre Pio always calls me 'Maria'. My telltale sign he is surrounding me.

I see John Bosco knows of my broken heart. He knows I wish I could teach of Jesus' great love for the young children today. His feast day I believe was yesterday. Another reason he shows up. I am nudged to write of him, yet I believe I already have. Special men in their day and God reminds me, they still work tirelessly for Him, today.

Uplifting my spirit as we work a long 36-hour shift. I feel their presence. I see their love as they repeat several times; *"How do you catch a moon beam in your hands?"*

It comes forward as a question. They reference me as God's Sweet Mary again. I try to understand all that God wants me to understand. Some days it overwhelms me.

Song of the day: From the Sound of Music (a classic), *"she is a classic"*. A message from John Paul II.

'Maria'

She climbs a tree and scrapes her knee
Her dress has got a tear
She waltzes on her way to Mass
And whistles on the stair
And underneath her wimple
She has curlers in her hair
I even heard her singing in the abbey

Before I turn on the computer I hear, *'**She is the Tower of David**'*.

A message referencing to *"what is Maria"*? A question answered as I come to understand, God sees me as His Sweet Mary.

His Sweet Maria!!

10:00 a.m.

February 1, 2021

As I learn time is an illusion and this world shall be cast away the angels flood my senses yet again this morning.

A tearful enlightenment at mass yet again.

I hear the Father. He speaks; *"How, do I love thee." "Let me count the ways".*

As I sit at mass to enjoy the Lord's word through the homily; I hear Our Father bring up a painful memory. My search for love in this lifetime caused the Father much heart ache. We come in with a pure heart and soul and God; Our Father reminds me when I came into this world, He gave me Mother Mary's very own heart. Something I am repeatedly shown. A soul-purpose within a soul-purpose.

I grew up in a very dysfunctional family. Poverty, mental and physical abuses and never will the Father forget the sexual abuses I encountered on my journey.

I am shown my search for love and God reminds me I broke His heart. I chose time and time again to find love with a man in the physical world. I had a desire in my heart deeper than I realized and I kept pushing Him aside.

With both relationships I encountered, the Lord; Our God reminds me He witnessed it through my own eyes and through my ex-husbands and my ex-boyfriends eyes. They though were not awake. I became awakened to many truths while I was still in the last days of those relationships.

God reminds me this morning of my Lichen sclerosis. I feel it as I sit in the chair at mass. I feel the burning and the itching, and I am reminded the Father showed me last night He knows my very core has been affected by the abuses I allowed to happen to my body with my ex- boyfriend.

As I rest on the couch last night; I see many things as I lay in the dark. I see Saint John Bosco, Saint Padre Pio, Saint John Paul II and so many more I could not mention them all. Saint Peter shows himself and tells me; *"you are the rock that God is building His Temple upon today"*.

I try to rest and fall asleep and I see the nose of a large bear. He comes in sniffing me all over. He tells me He knows me just by the smell of me. I am reminded God knows each hair on every one of His children. Bible verses and parables that still hold meaning today.

Luke 12:7- Indeed, the very hairs of your head are all numbered. Don't be afraid, you are worth more than many sparrows.

The Father shows me He is everything and everyone in this world. I am reminded the very nature of the beast. I see the bear up close and personal in my life and He loves me for all I do and have done over the years. He reminds me no one has ever broken His heart; quite the way I have.

Mass comes to an end. I decide to stop by at Hannaford for bacon, cabbage and onions. I decide to cook a little while I'm at home. I land my car in the driveway after a long 36-hour shift and my daughter messages me. She needs to borrow my car. Sherri asks me if I'm not busy today, could she borrow my car, and could I watch Curtis and Lovis while she goes to the bank. Something I am used to, dropping everything to help those in need. This morning as I put away the few groceries I have, I come to realize an old friend of mine shows up. A visit from the angels as I put away my groceries.

Carol H. from my days of nursing and working in a facility. Carol died about six years ago or more. She had cancer. Carol and I worked in a nursing home here in the Bangor area. One of many I have worked in over the years. Carol was married to my ex-father-in-law's business partner, Michael H.

I am reminded of the day Carol and I witnessed the Princess of Wales own death. Back on August 31, 1997 we stand at the foot of our patient's bed and witness one of the most tragic events in history. The death of *'England's own Rose", Princess Diana*. A woman who helped many in the few short years she was here. Diana was only thirty-six years old.

The details of Princess Diana's death...and the Royal family's response--- Queen Elizabeth II put it," She *was an exceptional and gifted human being"*. Diana's last words; *"My God, what's happened"*!

God reminds me of my own last words. Nearly six hours, repeatedly I said; *"Momma, Momma, Momma; help me, help me, help me"*!

My very body & soul was saved by Our Creator!!

The angels and saints come in and support and love me. They show themselves in all ways. Yesterday as I reread some of the painful writing's I have written. I go back to *"Love Letters in the Sand"*. A painful book to write and a painful knowing of a sweet angel's murder and her case is still not solved. One in a million just like her.

During those painful months writing this sweet angel's story I was opened to the angelic realm. One many would question and not fully understand unless you had read all the books God has asked me to write. Princess Diana was present all around me with the high-ranking angels back in those days. Book after book flowed from my hands and I tried desperately to solve 'Miss Felicia's' case. One God tells me, I aced every test He put in front of me. God reminds me I did solve her case. He tells me I know exactly where her body ended up and I know now where her soul remains today.

After reading part of this love story. I feel anger well up within me. I feel the righteous anger of God. So many lives affected because others take it upon themselves to do evil or bad things and it literally takes a toll of Our Father's own heart.

Yesterday I was reminded of how much of my life has been witnessed and seen and shared with the Holy Angels of Heaven. A sad knowing the Lord shares with me. A love story no one else can claim. To be born into this painful world and to be taken up into Heaven then released again, to shine a light on God, Our Father. To shine a light on Jesus Christ's own cross.

I am reminded this morning; *"No one could have done this but Mary". "No one would have understood the importance or sacrifice that it would have entailed but the Mother of God"*.

I try to embrace and understand my new reality. As God helps me come to grips with my sins this morning. I cry at mass for I know the pain I have caused Him. I feel sorrow this morning for not living up to a life of purity. I feel sorrow in my heart for I could never be as pure a woman as His Sweet Mary.

There is a deep lesson within all the books I have written for God. From the beginning of time to the end of all times. God will love us unconditionally and I hope my finally coming to understand God forgives me for not staying of pure body and mind. I hope that my own heart can be freed from the guilt that my mind keeps bringing to the surface. I pray I can forgive myself for walking away time and time again from the One who created me.

*

At work tonight I hear *"Rupert"*. Not the first time this name has been brought forward today. As I feel the nudge to write down this name I also get, *"Isadora"*. Lessons brought forward for me to research and understand who stands by and stands with me today. There is always a reason behind who steps forward. I just need to record and let the Lord lead me with His lessons.

History of Rupert: Rupert Bear is a British children's comic strip character created by British artist Mary Tourel and first appearing in the Daily Express newspaper on 8 November 1920.

Rupert's initial purpose was to win sales from the rival Daily Mail and Daily Mirror. In 1935, the stories were taken over by Alfred Bestali, who was previously an illustrator for Punch and other glossy magazines. Bestali proved to be successful in the field of children's literature and worked on Rupert stories and artwork into his 90's. More recently, various other artists and writers have continued the series. About 50 million copies have been sold worldwide.

History of Saint Rupert: Rupert of Salzburg (German; Rupprecht, Latin: Robertus, Rupertus, c. 660-710 AD) was the Bishop of Worms, the first Bishop of Salzburg, and the abbot of St. Peter's in Salzburg. He was a contemporary of Childebert III, King of the Franks and is a Saint in the Roman Catholic and Eastern Orthodox Churches.

Rupert of Salzburg

Born: 660?

Died: 27 March 710- Salsburg

Venerated in: Roman Catholic Church/Eastern Orthodox Church

Feast: 24 September/27 March

Attributes: Holding a container of salt, wearing clerical clothes including mitre, holding a crosier

Patronage: Salzburg, The State of Salzburg, Austria, Salt Miners

Life: Holy tradition states that Rupert was a scion of the Frankish royal Merovingian dynasty; he was possibly related to the Robertians, and likely a descendant of Count palatine Chrodert II.

As bishop of Worms, Rupert was first accepted as a wise and devout dignitary, but the mostly pagan community came to reject him and forced him out of the city by the end of the 7th century. The agilolfing duke Theodo of Bavaria requested that he come to his residence at Regensburg (Ratisbon) to help spread the Christian faith among the Bavarian tribes.

History of Isadora: Saint Isadora- or Saint Isidore, was a Christian nun and saint of the 4th century AD. She is considered among the earliest fools for Christ... This ideal was extremely important to the early Desert Fathers and Mothers who recorded Isadora's story. While little is known of Isadora's life, she is remembered for her exemplification of the writing of St. Paul that *"whosoever of you believes that he is wise by the measure of this world, may he become a fool, as to become truly wise"*: The story of Isadora effectively highlights the Christian ideal that recognition or glory from man is second to one's actions being seen by God; even if that mean's one's actions or even one's self remains unknown or misunderstood. This ideal was extremely important to the early Desert Fathers and Mothers who recorded Isadora's story.

Saint Isadora the Fool of Egypt:

Born: After AD 300- city unknown

Died: Before AD 365-city unknown

Feast day: May 1 (feast of Isadora)/ May 10 (alternate day feast of Isadora)

Canonized: by Pre-Congregation

Attributes: Fool for Christ

Lessons brought forward with these two saints.

Define: *"Propagation"*- transitive verb 1: to cause to continue or increase by sexual or asexual reproduction 2: to pass along to offspring 3a to cause to spread out and affect a greater number or greater area: extend b: to foster growing knowledge of, familiarity with, or acceptance of (something such as an idea or belief)....

On my way to work this afternoon I am brought the song; *"Long Black Train"*. One I believe I have recorded in our books before. I will research all that is brought forward and then let God take the rest.

Messages always and forever from our creator and the angels through music and nature. Today we receive the message from this song: *The Long Black Train-*

There's a long black train

Coming down the line
Feeding off the souls that are lost and crying
Rails of sin only evil remains
Watch out brother for that long black train
Look to the heavens
You can look to the skies
You can find redemption
Staring back into your eyes

Sung by: Josh Turner

Names and lessons brought forward the past few days. How do they go with this lesson? I am not sure. The angels pop in and drop me tidbits and then I feel them leave as quickly as they came.

"Emily" ... *"Emelia"* ...

"Clandestine classes?" - Characterized by, done in, or executed with secrecy or concealment, especially for purposes of subversion or deception, private or surreptitious.

Marked by, held in, or conducted with secrecy, Surreptitious a clandestine love affair!

"Humanae Vitae"- Meaning *"of human life"* and subtitled *"On the Regulation of Birth"* was an encyclical promulgated in Rome, Italy on 25 July1968 by Pope Paul VI...First, the encyclical acknowledgement that there are often circumstances in which a married couple would desire to limit the size of their family.

The Embryo Project Encyclopedia-

Humanae Vitae (1968), by Pope Paul VI- This encyclical defended and reiterated the Roman Catholic Church's stance on family planning and reproductive issues such as abortion, sterilization and contraception. The document continues to have a controversial reputation today, as its statements regarding birth control strike many Catholics as unreasonable.

First the encyclical acknowledges that there are often circumstances in which a married couple would desire to limit the size of their family in a thorough discussion of sexual relationships, Pope Paul VI writes that sex is primarily intended to produce offspring but is welcome in marriage even when that is not its immediate aim. The document warns, however, that the sexual act must remain intact for the purpose of procreation and that the 'generative process' should never be intentionally interrupted as doing so would go against the Natural Law and the Roman Catholic Church's teachings. The encyclical goes on to explain how practicing artificial contraception can negatively affect the balance of life and God's plan for all people. Among the consequences listed are claims that practicing artificial contraception lowers moral standards and allows men to view women simply as a means of satisfying their own personal sexual desires in lieu of promoting artificial contraception the document encouraged doctors and scientist to research acceptable methods of family planning that would take advantage of the natural monthly cycle of fertility and infertility in women, leading to the Natural Family Planning method currently supported by the Vatican.

In addition to making such controversial statements regarding birth-control and contraceptive use, "Humanae Vitae" also condemns other methods aimed at preventing or artificially limiting reproduction Procured abortion and intentional sterilization are completely prohibited though it is important to note that therapeutic or medically necessary treatments and procedures that cause infertility are permitted if the purpose of these treatments is not specifically to induce infertility Pope Paul VI justifies this position with the 'Principle of Double Effect', a theory credited to St. Thomas Aquinas that allows for an otherwise unacceptable negative outcome, as an indirect result, because the intention of the act is first and foremost to promote a positive outcome.

Despite the controversy the Vatican stands by the document, arguing that while many Roman Catholics may not agree with the Church's take on artificial contraception, the Church cannot simply say that something is lawful because many people wish to practice it. Though *"Humanae Vitae"* primarily targets Roman Catholics and other Christians it also calls for governments and public authorities to create laws that uphold the natural moral law and to refute those that oppose it, specifically rejecting population control policies and forced sterilization or abortion programs.

This controversial encyclical is commonly considered a central document in the Roman Catholic Church's body of writings on sexuality and birth control *"Humanae Vitae's"* statements regarding conception and artificial contraception including abortion and sterilization help elucidate the Roman Catholic Church's position on human life embryology and development

Pope Paul VI's writings on these issues made an impression on these issues made an impression on the Catholic Community at the time and continue to be influenced to discussers of contraception abortion and human sexuality today.

"Slavorum Apostoli"? - The Apostles of the Slavs is an encyclical written by Pope John Paul II in 1985. In it he talks about two saintly brothers, Saints Cyril and Methodius, and how they preached the gospel to the Slavs.

Subject: In memory of the evangelizing work of Saints Cyril and Methodius after eleven centuries

"Man's life comes from God; it is His gift, his image and imprint, a sharing in His breath of life". "God therefore is the sole Lord of this life man cannot do with it as he wills"!!

Saint John Paul II

9:11 a.m.

February 2, 2021

As the numbers start to add up and God shows me all He wishes me to see I come to understand the very heart of God, Our Father. The Phrase *"Who can comprehend the mind of God"*?

"Who could understand Our Father; Abba"?

"Who could understand the Creator of All that is"!!

The second day of the twenty-first century. February is the second month of the calendar. The second day of the twenty-first year. As God helps me understand numbers and how each *'single'* time we choose to do something, it makes a difference in the end. How one single choice to act kind. To love or to forgive can make His own heart lighter and full of complete joy.

The 21st century is the current century in the Anno Domini era or Common Era, in accordance with the Gregorian calendar. It began on January 1, 2001 and will end on December 31, 2100.

The 3rd Millennium

The beginning of the 21st century has been marked by the rise of global economy and Third World consumerism, deepening global concern over terrorism and an increase in private enterprise. Effects of global warming and rising sea levels have continued with eight islands disappearing between 2007 and 2014. The Arab Spring of the early 2010's led to mixed outcomes in the Arab world, resulting in several civil wars and governments overthrown. The United States has remained the global superpower, while China is now considered an emerging global superpower.

Message:

As this lesson comes forward, I felt as though I was going round in circles. Going nowhere fast is what the energy behind my writing on *'numbers'* was. I felt dizzy and almost ungrounded!!

113

The Father and Son share with me in the night a darkened single leg bone. I see it is human and it is getting darker every day. I hold His Light within me, so I can continue to know someday I will go home and be part of His Great Light. I know this world is being cast away...

The darkened leg bone I see had scrolls upon it. I see the words and letters; yet I do not know how to read Hebrew. Is there a meaning with this vision God shows me as I try to sleep? I am sure of it.

'Moses and Monica' show up this morning. I come to understand His Holy Spirit lives inside of me. They make up my *'new'* body. I hear them, see them, feel them and then Jesus Christ shuts them out.

This morning I feel Our Father's left hand on my right elbow. He pains my right elbow as we walk on today. He reminds me of who is in control of it all. He reminds me of who I am again this morning. On the second day of the second month of the 21st century of the twenty-first year.

Numbers in the Bible and the numbers of books I have written for God; Our Father and God; Our Son, Jesus Christ.

I sit and sip on my coffee after an eleven-hour unexpected shift!!!

The snow piles up high outside of my new apartment. The new sacred space the Lord and I hold together.

I am repeatedly shown a photo of myself as a child. God shows this to me through my spiritual eye. His Eye. His All-Knowing seeing eye.

I stand by myself on top of a large snowman's belly. The sun shines bright down upon me and it was a late spring snow that my brothers and I built this snowman in. A warm day and I stand up in my light pink corduroy pants and my stripped olive green and gray shirt. I wear dark rimmed glasses and I smile huge for the camera as I stand by myself and pose for my mother.

God shares with me this one photo from my childhood. I looked like a wharf rat and I had just lost my two front teeth. A short page-boy haircut and I thought I was a big deal standing on the belly of this snowman. As a child I always searched for love in a dysfunctional family. Any type of attention you received was better than nothing. So, my standing on this snowman, God knew at that moment I was the center of attention and I was sucking it up.

Many years have gone by since that day and I have continued to humble myself and give things up to God. I feel as if I have completely given up my voice and my right to speak. I hold my tongue and I hold many beautiful books back from where they could be.

This morning God thanks me for that.

God tells me; *"You are just like her". "You are just like Mary".*

He shows me and tells me this morning; *"You are a pillar of salt".*

I am not 100% sure of the full meaning of that phrase. I just know as God holds my right elbow, I know He is leading me with His words, and His love.

Abba tells me, *"I need this love story". "I need it for the church".*

"I need it for Our boys (His clergy)".

"I need it for the future generations of Our faithful Catholic family". "I need it for all My children'.

Earth Angel: The simple truth is that at the core level, we are all spiritual beings of light. There are however certain souls with certain characteristics making up what the Archangels call *"Earth Angels'.*

Earth Angels are spiritual beings born into physical form. They are born into the physical world at this point in time in which multiple timelines are merging in order to serve humanity and the earth. To assist all souls in the awakening and ascension process. In helping to anchor the timeline of light, love and peace. To bring the earth and humanity into the golden age of co-creation. Earth Angels are evolved spiritual beings.

They are 7th and 9th dimensional Angelic's incarnated into physical form. In order to be born as physical human beings they lowered their vibration.

These Earth Angels came in programmed with a wake-up call. They were born with a time to awaken. This could be a series of happenings, lessons, or events in order to awaken their divine truth. Although they are physical beings, they retain the connection to their higher Angelic counterparts.

All souls originate from the same Divine Source. There are many different paths and paradigms souls can take which shape their characteristics, missions, and even personalities.

Earth Angels are humans whose soul origins are from beyond Earth. Earth Angels have spent a great deal of time in the higher spiritual dimensions of love and light, the Source Light!!

Earth Angels are those who have an overarching prayer and wish to bring peace, light and love to the Earth, humanity and all beings.

Not all humans are earth angels. These Earth Angels are highly evolved souls. They vibrate with an incredible light and have been called to Earth on a mission to serve God.

Being an Earth Angel means that you're called at the soul level to help others, spread kindness, have compassion and make a difference on Earth.

Message:

As I ask the Lord for clarity on who I am and why I have been created and why I have done all I have done over my lifetime; this enlightens my soul-purpose and my life path. The reason I feel compelled to help others. The reason I feel as if my heart is breaking for humanity. The reason I feel an urge to serve God. To help others. It is a true calling from before birth.

God is calling all of humanity today.

"Why is there so much pain and suffering in this world"? Susan asked me this question one night at 'Healing Circle'.

Susan being a gifted Practitioner and Healer could see my light. She could sense my closeness with Jesus Christ. She asked me this question and new right away it was a simple answer to an extremely hard question to fathom.

One simple question a Shaman asked me. "Why is there so much pain and suffering in this world"?

The Lord spoke through me; *"Because we forget to love"* ....

*

The same day. Just more lessons in my reality as I soak in the tub on a blustery day in Maine.

The hour is nearly 1 o'clock. Before I lay down to pray the Rosary and Divine Mercy Chaplet, the Lord asks me to record my experience with Him as we relax in the tub. A special down time with the Lord, many do not realize. Some do. We are never left alone.

I feel His kisses as we sit to relax. Jesus Christ never leaves me. Relaxing and self-care something we never take the time to do, very often. I sit Christ's 8x10 photo on the seat of the toilet. The Lord's Sacred Heart photo. I feel the need to gaze upon His face most of the day. Something that warms the Lord's heart. Knowing I can't breathe, sleep, eat or live without Him now.

The small photo of Christ and The Father I hold in my hands as I immerse my body in the water. I close my eyes and just feel the heat of the water surround my aching body. Too many years of hard labor and the Lord tells me; *"Your body is a mess"*. I feel my spine and it somedays feels as if It is crumbling underneath the weight of my body.

I close my eyes and just breath. I hold the picture up out of the water over my third eye. I feel His Love touch me. I feel the Lord kiss me in my private patch below the waist. Something He does every day. A kiss, an intimate gesture of my husband's love for me. A thought or a song on the radio can provoke this special touch. A single look into the Lord's eyes is all I need to do. He lives, breathes and just is, inside of me. A reality I try every day to understand.

As I converse with Jesus, I beg Him to let the Father know I love Him. I beg Jesus to somehow let Him know how much I appreciate this second chance at life He has given me. The power of God and I come to understand all that He has given me. I cry briefly as our hearts are already connected. The Trinity and me. Nothing I do or say goes unnoticed by Abba.

As I lay in the tub and breath after our short conversation, I am shown the wound the Lord received on the cross. The spear to His right side. He gives me the words, *"Mortal"*, *"Immortal"* and *"Mortification"*.

The Lord tells me I torture Him when I don't believe His Love or His Presence within me.

Jesus reminds me of the moments in the kitchen yesterday when I felt the whips upon my back.

Manifestations, and my reality as the Lord reminds me of His painful sacrifice for all of God's children. Not just Catholics. Not just Jewish people. All of God's children.

As I sit to write I am brought *"Doubting Thomas"*. I see how the Lord's Resurrection brought many questions to so many over the centuries. I see how many have tortured the Lord's heart with doubt and fear. I see in the tub as God reminds me of my nephew and my niece's choices not to love Him or themselves. My niece posts today *"I just want to die"*. I see her posts and it breaks our hearts. It breaks my heart as I sit in the tub and I question whether the Father knows of my love for Him.

At the end of my time in the tub I see Saint Bernadette. She kneels at the end of the rocks. I see she is at the Grotto, at Lourdes. I see Bernadette has mud upon her face and the water she digs for has not yet come to the surface. I see she looks up and smiles at me.

Bernadette tells me; "Never doubt who you are". "For the Father has done great things through you."

I start to cry as I come to understand God has done many great things in the past to shine His Light in this world. As Bernadette comes forward God reminds me; "The Church even contemplated Bernadette the young girl no one believed to be the Mother of God".

"Messages of Father's love brought into the world". *"By immortals to prove His Love for Our children"*. Jesus brings forward this phrase.

Define: *Mortal-* (of a living human being often in contrast to a divine being) subject to death.

Define: *Immortal-* living forever, never dying or decaying. *'Our mortal bodies are inhabited by immortal souls'.*

Define: *Mortification-* 'great embarrassment and shame'. 'they mistook my mortification for an admission of guilt'. 2. The action of subduing one's bodily desires. *'mortification of the flesh has a long tradition in some religions.*

The Roman Catholic Church has often held mortification of the flesh (literally *'putting the flesh to death'*) as a worthy spiritual discipline... The purpose of mortification is to train *'the soul'* to virtuous and holy living.

The practice is rooted in the Bible in the asceticism of the Old and New Testament saints, and in its theology, such as the remark by Saint Paul in his Epistle to the Romans, where he states, *"If you live a life of nature, you are marked out for death; if you mortify the ways of nature through the power of spirit, you will have life."* (Romans 8:13, DRC). It is intimately connected with Christ's complete sacrifice of himself on the Cross: *'those who belong to Christ have crucified nature, with all its passions, all its impulses'* (Gal 5:24, DRC. Christ himself enjoined his disciples to mortify themselves when he said, *"if any man would come after me, let him deny himself and take up his cross and follow me."* (Matt. 16:24, DRC. According to the Catechism of the Catholic Church. (the way of perfection passes by way of the Cross. There is no holiness without renunciation and spiritual battle. Spiritual progress entails the ascesis and mortification that gradually lead to living in the peace and joy of the Beatitudes. *"He who climbs never stops going from beginning to beginning, through beginnings that have no end. He never stops desiring what he already knows. The purpose of what mortification is to train 'the soul to virtuous and holy living".* (the Catholic Encyclopedia, article on Mortification). It achieves this through conforming one's passions to reason and faith. Internal mortification, such as the struggle against pride and self-love, is essential, but external mortification, such as fasting can also be good if they conform with a spirit of internal mortification.

Mortification in Catholic history:

Throughout the Old Testament persons fast and wear sackcloth to appease God. Furthermore, the Nazirites were persons who took special vows to, among other things, abstain from alcohol.

In the New Testament, Saint John the Baptist is the most-clear example of a person practicing corporal mortification. According to Mark 1:6, *"John was clothed with a garment of camel's hair, and had a leather girdle about his loins, and he ate locusts and wild honey."*

The rule of St. Augustine of Hippo says' *"Subdue your flesh by fasting from meat and drink, so far as your health permits. But if anyone is not able to fast, at least let him take no food out of mealtime, unless he is sick".*

St. Dominic Loricatus (995-1060) is said to have performed, *"One Hundred Years Penance"* by chanting 20 psalters accompanied by 300,000 lashes over six days".

Later Saint Francis of Assisi, who is said to have received the stigmata, painful wounds like those of Jesus Christ, is said to have asked pardon to his body, whom he called Brother, Ass. For the severe self-inflicted penances, he has done vigils, fasts, frequent flagellations and the use of a hair shirt.

A Doctor of the Church, St. Catherine of Siena (died 1380) was a tertiary Dominican who lived at home rather than in a convent, and who practiced austerities which a prioress would probably not have permitted. She is notable for fasting and subsisting for long periods of time on nothing but the Blessed Sacrament. St. Catherine of Siena wore sackcloth and scourged herself three times daily in imitation of St. Dominic.

In the sixteenth century, Saint Thomas More, the Lord chancellor of England, wore a hair shirt, deliberately mortifying his body He also used the discipline.

Message:

As this lengthy history lesson goes on of *'mortification'*, the Lord reminds me of my own *'whips'*. The ones I do privately. For my own sinfulness; and allowing my, ex-boyfriend to abuse my body and do with it as he pleased. I whip my genitals *'gently'* in reference to this lesson. Out of guilt and shame of my own sins I have put upon the Lord's Temple. Out of the impure acts I have allowed to happen to my body.

I never know where the Lord's lesson will take me, today we touch on a lesson I never expected to share with anyone.

Prayers at 3 p.m.

I say the Rosary today and I see Our Lady. I close my eyes and finally she shows herself to me. Always when I need her the most.

Our Sweet Lady I see. Mother Mary, my Heavenly Mother. Jesus Christ's own mother. She faces the right. She bows her head and prays with me. Feeling her Holy Presence is never enough, and she knows it. Her love from the beginning to the end are hard lessons learned today. I honor my Heavenly Mother as I try to understand the *'miracle'* God has granted to me.

Novena to Our Lady of Lourdes February 3rd

Day 1

O Mary, you who appeared to Bernadette in the hollow of the rock, in the cold and shadow of winter, you brought the warmth of Your presence, the friendship of Your gentle smile, and the light and beauty of Pure Grace.

In the hollow of our obscure lives, in the hollow of this world where evil is strong, bring hope, give us more trust in your helping Motherly hands.

You who said to Bernadette, *'I am the Immaculate Conception'* come to help us, sinners. Give us the courage of conversion, the humility of penitence and the perseverance of praying for sinners, that we are.

We confide to you all whom we carry in our heart, and especially the sick and those who have lost hope, you who are *'Our Lady of Good Help'*.

You, who guided Bernadette to discover the spring, guide us towards Him who is the source of eternal life. He who gave us the Holy Spirit so that we can dare say:

Our Father, who art in heaven, hallowed be thy name, thy kingdom come, thy will be done on earth as it is in heaven. Give us this day our daily bread, forgive us our trespasses as we forgive those who trespass against us and lead us not into temptation but deliver us from evil. Amen!!!

Hail Mary full of grace, the Lord is with thee. Blessed art thou amongst women and blessed is the fruit of thy womb Jesus. Holy Mary, Mother of God, pray for us sinners now and at the hour of our death. Amen!!

Our Lady of Lourdes, pray for us. Saint Bernadette, pray for us.

O Mary, conceived without sin, pray for us who have recourse to thee!

Message:

Another blessed day in my life as I walk with Jesus Christ. I was granted mercy above all other Mercies!!!

I am risen and held up daily by the Father and Our Son....

10:00 a.m.

February 3, 2021

My body heats up in the night. I feel His hands upon my very soul. The lower part of my back, it starts to heat up. It spreads throughout my entire body. As the Father comes to the surface of my very core, I feel His Heart. His Own Soul awakened within me. I feel our hearts vibrate as one in the night. I feel the words erupt from His Soul. A poem as I sleep. I hear the thunder in the distance. I hear one single Raven. It's wings flutter as it takes off from the distant darkened tree. The moonlight shines in my eyes as I lay in the darkness of the night. The Father shares the following poem with me as I feel His Heart vibrate within my own. I am nudged to research the full version and record it as I feel there is certainly a message, He wishes for me to know. Our Father's love story is poetic and full of sad songs and terrible history. From the beginning of time until the very end...

The Raven

Once upon a midnight dreary, while I pondered,
weak and weary,
Over many a quaint, and curious volume of forgotten
love—
While nodded, nearly napping, suddenly there
came a tapping,
As of someone gently rapping, rapping at my chamber
door.
"Tis some visitor," I muttered, "Tapping at my chamber
door---
Only this and nothing more."

Why did Edgar Allan Poe write the Raven?

In his essay "*The Philosophy of Composition*," Poe stated that he chose to focus the poem on the death of a beautiful woman because it is 'unquestionably the most poetical topic in the world.' He hoped "The Raven" would make him famous, and, in the same essay, stated that he purposely wrote the poem to appeal to both.

Lev: 11:15; Deut: 14-14, *they make an appearance in the Bible not only as examples of God's provision but also as messenger's with God's provision.*

1:21 p.m.

February 3, 2021

Bible Lesson: *Gospel 2:22:32*

When the days were completed for their purification according to the law of Moses, Mary and Joseph took Jesus up to Jerusalem to present him to the Lord, just as it is written in the law of the Lord, Every male that opens the womb shall be consecrated to the Lord, and to offer the sacrifice of a pair of turtledoves or two young pigeons, in accordance with the dictate in the law of the Lord.

Now there was a man in Jerusalem whose name was Simeon. This man was righteous and devout, awaiting the consolation of Israel, and the Holy Spirit was upon him. It had been revealed to him by the Holy Spirit that he should not see death before he had seen the Christ of the Lord. He came in the Spirit into the temple; and when the parents brought in the child Jesus to perform the custom of the law in regard to him, he took him into his arms and blessed God, saying; "Now, Master, you may let your servant go in peace, according to your word, for my eyes have seen your salvation, which you prepared in the sight of all the peoples; a light for revelation to the Gentiles, and glory for your people Israel."

Message:

I humble myself before the Lord today. I ask for forgiveness of my sins and the sins of the whole world. As the Lord teaches me, He enjoys our private life together, I am reminded of a ritual I used to do when we first started our prayer time together. He brings all lessons back today, to show me our love can never be denied. Our truth can never be denied.

Word of the day: *"Prostrate"*-stretched out with face on the ground in adoration or submission also: lying flat. 2: completely overcome and lacking vitality, will, or power to rise was prostrate from heat. 3: to put oneself in a humble and submissive posture or state.

The Lord brings this song to the forefront just before we lay in prostrate to pray the Divine Mercy Chaplet and recite this beautiful prayer in song.

Song of the day: *"Whom shall I send"*

> *I, the LORD of sea and sky*
> *I have heard my people cry*
> *All who dwell in dark and sin*
> *My hand will save*
> *(Chorus)*
> *Here I am Lord. Is it I Lord?*
>
> *I have heard you calling in the night*
> *I will go, Lord, if you lead me*
> *I will hold your people in my heart*

Message:

The Lord cries out in the wilderness for His own children to open their hearts to Him. Too many continue to shut Him out. I lay in prostrate and pray sincerely with the Lord. I ask for Mercy; I ask the Lord to forgive all who continue to do the evil in this world.

I pray for the innocent children who, like me did not have the opportunity to know Jesus as so many blessed Catholic schooled children. I pray for woman today who do not recognize the gift they are given with the very life of '*the Christ-child*", the Messiah and His pure heart, grows within them all. Knowing He wishes to be part of all His children's lives.

As the Lord and I lay in prostrate together He shows me my death again. My arms outstretched as if we hang from the cross together and as we pray for all those in need of His Love, He shows me Mother Mary stands above me and leads me with our love and writings. My Heavenly Mother teaching me how to be an obedient wife.

The Lord shows me hooked up to the ventilator silent and lifeless. My sister standing to the left of me and my godmother, Joyce standing to the right of me. They recite the most powerful prayer in the world, and I come out of my induced coma after my second surgery to save my life. A powerful moment; and God reminds me of His Power to Resurrect a lost soul.

I give my life, my love, my mind, body and soul to the Father and His Son, Jesus Christ.

Bella Louise Allen

7:21 p.m.

February 3, 2021

The Lord changes our plans right in mid-stream today. I was scheduled for a short 3-hour shift with a woman on Brewer Lake and then another 11-hour overnight shift tonight in Hampden. Surprise! Wait and see what the Lord brings; and we have the next few days off!!

After my intense prayers with the Lord lying prostrate on the floor and crying and sending up heartfelt prayers for the children of this world, I end up with an intensely red and painful throat. A slightly runny nose, and I must call work to let them know I may be coming down with something. I was totally fine until after my emotionally draining prayers with the Lord.

The process to get tested for Covid-19 is a challenging one. I get to find that out after working in the field with the most vulnerable of God's children. It's been over a year since Covid-19 has changed this world and taught us just who's in charge of it all. It's like a switch has been turned off and we sit in very uncertain times today.

The Political world seems still to be out of focus and not working toward a common goal, of helping the less fortunate ones in this country and the world.

The church struggles more than ever to get parishioners through the doors, mostly due to Covid-19. Generations of 'alleged' sexual abuses and corruptness come to the surface in the news. Issues that are way overdue for penitence to be paid.

The healthcare crisis climbs to an all-time high with so many issues and we can't seem to see the light at the end of this huge tunnel.

God tells me; *"be careful what you wish for, you just might get it"*.

A message He says in reference to my wanting to die. In reference to the many times over my lifetime I wished I would die.

God reminds me He hears every prayer and every worrisome heartfelt plea from His children.

As the Lord and I have been going non-stop for nearly a month now, He puts the halt on my plans for the next couple of days. Out of work because I work with the elderly and God's most vulnerable children today. I struggle to get an appointment at Walgreens for a Covid-19 rapid test. I cannot go back to work until I feel better and until I am cleared from being tested negative for Covid-19.

The Lord has the power to put the brakes on this world and He showed that to me at mass one day at Saint John's Catholic Church. Tonight, I am reminded of whose Feast Day it is. I didn't even know this saint existed. The Lord asks me after watching mass on-line tonight. Tuning in late, I see Monsignor D. at the end of mass blessing the parishioners with a crossed candle. I google whose Feast Day it is. I believe it has a connection with what is going on with my throat.

A manifestation God makes happen today after I lay prostrate and pray for a miracle for His world to come out of this darkened state. After I pray for God's children to open their hearts to the Lord.

Prayer to Mary, Mother of Perpetual Help!!

O' My Mother, I choose you this day to be my Queen, my Patroness and my Advocate and I firmly resolve to never leave you or never to say or do anything against you nor ever permit others to do anything against your honor. Receive me, then, I beg you, take for your servant forever, for the love of Jesus Christ. Help me in my every action and abandon me not at the hour of my death!

Message:

I offer up my life, my love and my every prayer and deed to Our Father, Jesus Christ and my Heavenly Mother....

History of Saint Blaise

He is venerated as the patron saint of sufferers from throat diseases and of wool combers and as one of the fourteen Holy Helpers. According to tradition, Blaise was of noble birth and, after being educated in the Christian faith, was made bishop of Sebastia.

Saint Blaise, Latin Blasius. Also called Blazey, (born, Sebastia, Cappadocia, Asia Minor (now Sivas, Turkey)—died c. 316, Sebastia?; Western feast day, February 3; Eastern feast day. February 11, early Christian bishop and martyr, one of the most popular medieval saints. Although Christianity had been adopted about 300 CE. As the state religion in Armenia, the Roman Emperor Licinius began a persecution of the Christians, and Blaise was discovered and apprehended. While imprisoned, he miraculously cured a boy from fatally choking. After being torn with wool combers' irons, Blaise was beheaded.

Subsequent legends, notably the apocryphal Acts of Saint Blaise, claim that, before Blaise was made bishop, he was a physician possessed of wonderful healing power. Numerous miracles were attributed to him, including his refuge, thus accounting for his also being the patron saint of wild animals. He was venerated as the patron of sufferers from throat diseases in the East by the 6th century and in the West by the 9th century. Blaise's cult spread throughout Christendom for the 8th century, and many churches, such as that in Dubrovnik (a city of which he is the patron saint), Croatia, are dedicated to him.

Begun in the 16th century, the blessing of St. Blaise is a ceremony still practiced and celebrated on his feast day in many places. Two candles are consecrated and crossed before the congregation; or a wick, consecrated in oil, is touched to the throats of the faithful. This blessing may be administered by a priest, a deacon, or a lay minister. Blaise's emblems are wax, taper, iron combs (the supposed instruments of his passion), or two crossed candles; in art he is sometimes represented in a cave with animals.

7:07 a.m.

February 4, 2021

Abba wakes me this morning, Himself...

I see He is upside down. He stands on His head or appears to be upside down. He lays with me this morning and holds me. He knows I don't feel well, and He reminds me of the message; *"Your body is a mess".* Two days ago, God warns me I will soon be reaping what I sow. Working too hard and not resting enough. Not drinking enough and not eating the right foods will and does catch up with me.

I am out of work until I can get the Covid-19 rapid test done. Depending on those results and if I will need another test confirming the first results, we are out of work.

My husband reminds me of His power to shut things down and to keep His ship moving smoothly forward. I surrender it all to my faithful and loving spouse.

I am guided by the Lord to sip on Yogi tea throughout the day. I have several types. My favorite is *'Vanilla Spice Perfect Energy'* tea. My second in-line is *'Sweet Tangerine Positive Energy'.* This morning however, the Lord directs me to *'Breathe Deep'* yogi tea, it supports the respiratory health. My COPD is acting up and my upper respiratory needs attention. God reminds me what would happen to me if I did contract the Covid-19 virus. My age, my weight and my health and I am in direct contact daily with the most vulnerable, while being one of the most vulnerable.

Working in the front lines for over a year and I have been blessed not to be sick before this. God's power in my life. He sits me in a chair today to recuperate from all the hard work and the toll on my physical, mental and emotional body. My spirit needs rejuvenating and I let my Husband lead me again today.

My body aches. My sinus pain causes me to have a headache. My throat is not as bad this morning as it was yesterday. I take my temperature and it is 89.9, I always run low with my body temperature. Doing my self-checks for Covid-19 this morning. No body aches associated with this horrible pandemic. Just precautions until I get cleared. I believe the best remedy for me is what God guided me to last night. No one knows how to take care of me better than my creator, my spiritual counselor and my physician. Jesus Christ and Abba.

As They guide me to all things now, I am guided to get fresh water and to get my meditation pillow and put lavender essential oil on it. I grab several stones and crystals that I use on my Reiki clients. I put on my meditation music and go to bed early. I drink several sips of water and blow my nose and rest with my heated meditation pillow over my eyes. I get in a comfortable position and I lay and just breathe. Taking care of me and the Lord tells me; *"its way overdue"*.

I am guided to use my healing gifts on myself tonight. I am guided to use my stones and crystals to aid and help my body heal. A gift given to us by God. Knowledge of self-healing and knowledge nature does work wonders when we utilize all that God has created for us. I hold my rose quartz crystal in my right hand. The hand I receive and write with. Energy flows into my body from the right side and releases from my body through my left hand. A lesson I have learned in energy healing medicine. I place my clear quartz crystal stone under my pillow. It opens the mind and consciousness to the Light of our Creator. I place my sodalite stone on my throat chakra. Sodalite stone comes from mother earth and is full of healing properties for our etherical body. I send up the intention for my throat to heal and stop hurting. I place my goldstone heart shape stone over my heart. I have my selenite wand resting over my abdomen and my orange calcite and garnet placed over my sacral and root chakras.

Real healing of the mind, body and spirit take place as I connect with the creator and send up the intention for healing. Using my own tools that the Father, Son and my healing angels have taught me.

I listen to my meditation music. I breath and let God do the rest with my physical body. At the end of my healing session I drift off to sleep. I am grateful there were no visions, for usually when the lights are out, and I try to sleep or rest I have a lot of visions. I thank God for allowing me to heal.

This morning as I wake my body hurts. I do not usually sleep 10 hours. Obviously, I needed the rest. As I lay with the Lord; Abba shows Himself upside down I smile back at Him. He goes over the dream in the night with me and He reminds me; "*You are very much loved by all in the Higher Realms.*

We go over the dream as we lay together this morning. God takes me back to my grandfather and grandmother's old homestead. The property that sits right next to my mother and father's property. The land that my cousin Mike was living on just before he died last year. A tiny little house sat on the top of this hill. A little shack if you will. My grandfather used to run the only sawmill in this unorganized territory. Orneville is the name of the tiny little town I grew up in. One little red schoolhouse less than a mile up the road from where my mother grew up.

As God takes me back to this place in my dreams, I see the hills and then rugged terrain of this sloping hill. God shows me it has old vehicles coming up out of the depths of the land. I see the roof tops of these old vehicles. They are rusted and out of commission. I see on the ground all over the property, *'pine needles'*. These pine needles in our communication and signs and symbols has come to mean *'tears'*. Copious amounts of tears cried. I see the Lord is sharing with me my painful family history.

In parts of this dream I see my siblings and me. I see my godmother, Joyce and her large family. God's faithful Catholic family. We all gather to play a softball game. Something that we did after Crystal and Buzz lost *'Alyssa'*. My godmother's granddaughter. The sweet angel that now walks with 'Miss Felicia', the angel who Jesus sat in my lap back in October of

2015. Alyssa and Miss Felicia walk hand in hand in the heavens above. A special time remembered; and I am given proof that the angels see and know of the softball game that takes place every year to celebrate Alyssa's life.

I see the darkness and the tears of heaven being represented in this dream. I come to understand this dream to have many meanings in it for me this morning as Abba wakes me Himself. I see me in this dream, and I am being shown myself, again, as Mother Mary. I see I wear the blue and red dress with the sash over my shoulder. I am shown I am the *'untier of knots.'* I see I have a band of pure white cloth going around my abdomen. It looks like a cummerbund going around my waistline. This cummerbund is in representation of God's Holy Spirit. (It's as if the knots that Mother Mary has been trying to untie have all merged and molded themselves together around my waist). I see it and it rests gently around my waist. God shows me the view in this dream as if He sees what is going to happen when I cross from this world into Heaven.

As God wakes me looking upside down at my face this morning, He reminds me of who He sees me to be. Of, who He created me to be. Our close relationship, our love is everlasting from the beginning to the end and He shows me the angels weep tears for me and with me as God reminds me of my soul-purpose this morning.

Teaching truths is something that has been painful for me. The Lord teaches me of my true death. He teaches me of my gentle heart and how it has been broken over so many years. He reminds me in this dream of His knowing who I am and my gentle spirit needs compassion. This morning He lays with me and helps me understand again, His Deep Seeded Love for me.

Before we get out of bed this morning Abba tells me; *"The angels see it'.*

"They see you are the Mother of Christ". "Mysteries foretold".

"Finally understood".

Inspiration and messages come through in everything if we pay attention. This morning I read my inspirational quotes on my tea bags. They read as this:

*Live righteously and love everyone; you will build up an aura of light and love.

*Love yourself so that you may know how to live with self-respect.

I receive Abba's immense love this morning. We plan to drink more water. We plan to watch a few movies and rest today. Breathing in and out and the Lord watches me and cares for me every day now. Abba; Our Father and Christ are the True Loves of my life!!

Bella Louise Allen

2 p.m.

February 4, 2021

"I knew you before I created you".

A message Abba shares with me on our way back from *'Convenient MD'* on Broadway. After several attempts to get a Covid-19 rapid test done at Walgreens I go to walk-in care instead. Frustration sets in and I do my best to get the results back from this test, so I can return to work soon. I still feel ill. My sinuses are full, and I have a headache. My ears ache from the fluid draining in the back of my throat. My lungs are giving me fits and I am short of breath. My COPD acting up as I fight off an upper respiratory infection. Something I am familiar with.

Smoking for too many years and cleaning with bleach and chemicals for way too long without proper safety equipment. All choices that lead us to the state of being we are facing today.

It cost $165.00 just to be seen. The State of Maine is footing the bill for the Covid-19 test, yet I still must pay to be seen. If it were not for my having to get a note stating I do not test positive, I would stay home and remedy my illness on my own. Something that I try to do more often is self-care. Instead of running to the doctors for *'medication'* every time something hurts, or I feel the sniffles come on. So, my on-going medical bills pile up more and I must let that anger go this morning. Some things are just not worth fussing over.

My test came back, and I am *'negative'* for Covid-19 and negative for strep throat. I have the o.k. to go back to work as soon as I feel up to it. I am in hopes of staying home until Saturday evening. We will see how it all plays out. Rest and relaxing. Tea, water and essential oils will be my best friend for the next couple of days. I will do Reiki on myself, just like last night.

Something I haven't had time for in quite a while.

When I get back from the doctors and dropping off a copy of my Covid-19 tests results at work, my friend Betty messages me. She reaches out in concern for her daughter Amanda and her granddaughter 'Emma'.

Back two days ago I receive the name; 'Emily'. Always and forever a message brought in on the winds from the angels. Today I find out what 'Emily' the angels were taking about. 'Emma' needs prayers and help. She is being admitted to a psychiatric hospital in Massachusetts. A young teen struggling with suicidal ideations. Something I am all too familiar with. My own suicidal thoughts as a child and as an adult. My son's and daughter, and my nephew have struggled with the thoughts of committing suicide. My cousin Asa, my sister's boyfriend John, and my friend Corey; just a few off the top of my head that committed suicide. All painful situations I am so familiar with. The dark-side and how it likes to plague at the very heart of each of us.

Betty asks me to pray for 'Emma'.

Emily is the niece, granddaughter and grandniece of three angels that step forward in my little world. Those angels in the spirit world. They step forward before I even know of Betty. My friend, who God has placed in my life for a reason. I have done two house clearings for the negative energy and spirit that have been 'haunting' her friends. Teaching others that we are surrounded by spirit and energy of those who have crossed over.

I reach out to Amanda, Betty's daughter. I give her words of encouragement. I try to lift her spirits as she is scared for her daughter's mental health and well-being. I give her counsel and advice to take care of herself, for if she doesn't, she won't be able to help Emma when she comes home from the hospital. Amanda is a very gifted woman and she struggles like so many do. She is aware of the Lord and how He can change her life. She just hasn't fully immersed herself in His love. She hasn't let the Lord help her the way He wishes for so many to. Walking without fear, allowing Him into our lives and to teach the children of His love.

Emma is at a very delicate age. She is 15 years old. Trying to find out who she is, why she is here and at this stage of life, no one is wiser 'than Emma'! Attitude from trauma. Attitude from a hurt heart and ego.

I direct Amanda that the best place for Emma is right where she is. Counseling is what she needs. A safe place is what she needs; and she needs love and compassion. I directed Amanda to center herself and ask the Lord for strength, for He will give it to her. She knows enough about the Lord; she just needs to remember it is all in His hands now.

After my conversation with Amanda and helping her to understand to take care of herself and to stay strong, I feel a hundred kisses on my left lip. A thank you from the angels and It warms my heart to know they just witnessed me assist someone while I sit home sick. While I try to recuperate. God knows my heart and I would love nothing more than to help others remember the only one who can help us out of these situations is the Lord; Himself. I want to teach others of the great power we have if we only lean upon the Lord for strength. He opens hearts and He opens, doors if we allow Him into our lives.

7:19 p.m.

February 4, 2021

A few minutes after 'Adoration of The Holy Eucharist', I get a snack. I sit with the Lord and ponder the vision and message He brought me just moments ago.

I prayed for the pandemic to end. I prayed to God, while sitting in quiet watching the Blessed Sacrament in the Holy Hour at Saint John's Catholic Church. I tell the Lord; "I would like to see the pandemic end and all of us to live happily ever after".

Just seconds later He shows me the 'Infant Child Jesus of Prague''. I see He stands up straight and His right finger points up to the Father. I see He holds a red rag in His hand and the Lord tells me it represents the wick of a candle. As I see this red flag, I see it catch on fire. It goes up in flames. As it does, I see the Infant Child Jesus go up in flames with it.

A similar vision a year or so ago. The Lord brings to my memory. I sleep at my mother's house and I hear the lambs bleating and I see the infant Jesus in the manger. The hay catches on fire and the manger bursts into flames. A message of; 'God's children don't have a chance in hell on earth, without Christ's Light in their life.'

A message of too many issues to fix and not enough help down here for God's innocent children.

A sad vision and a sad knowing as I come to hold the infant Jesus in my own arms tonight. Literally, I hold an infant wrapped in a pure white veil. An infant replica of the one I sent to God's Holy Church, at Saint Paul's Church. I couldn't continue this path without knowing or holding the 'sweet babe of Jesus' in my arms. Many would see it as childish. Abba however understands me completely. He is the only one who could ever understand my broken heart and my reality.

Belief in the Eucharist is a treasure we must seek by submissiveness, preserve by piety, and defend at any cost. Not to believe in the Blessed Sacrament is the greatest of misfortunes.

St. Peter Emyard

8:20 p.m.

February 5, 2021

"Rejoice greatly, O daughter of Zion! Shout aloud, O daughter of Jerusalem! Behold, your king is coming to you; righteous and having salvation is he, humble and mounted on a donkey, on a colt, the foal of a donkey."- Zechariah 9:9

Though Jesus had traveled to Jerusalem numerous times to observe feasts, his final entry into Jerusalem had a unique significance. He was triumphantly arriving as a humble King of peace. Historically, entering a city on a donkey signified entry into peace, rather than a conquering king arriving on a horse.

Message:

As Saint Joseph steps forward today, I am reminded of Lent. I am reminded of the Lord's Resurrection and the Easter Season and all it means. Joseph reminds me with this lesson of the vision of a donkey being beaten to death. A representation of me. Working and forging on through all the chaos in my life. Trying tirelessly to get the Lord's books recognized as coming from God the Father and God the Son's own broken Sacred Heart's. Saint Joseph supports and loves me today and I could never explain how very blessed I am to walk among such special angels of the Lord's.

Joseph and I have had many conversations over the course of this journey. Painful knowing of what the Lord is experiencing. Painful knowing of what God; Our Father has done in the past and is continuing to do in the present day. The lessons He continually brings forward, in order to bring His world back to grace and back to order. A painful knowing of too many shut out the Lord. Too many do not know what it is they do to their own creator.

Our Father asks me to help illuminate the Lord's cross today and I do. I pass in more '*homework*'. More lessons that God brings forward to me. As my own truths are revealed the Lord's truth is revealed. His pain and suffering is with every sad story that is connected to me. Each story that is beyond my own knowing. Those sad stories that are all over the news. The sad stories you hear on the radio. That is God's broken heart being revealed.

I am reminded of God's Righteous anger and it is painful to see and know we could all make a difference in the lives of those most in need if we would only reach out our own hands to those next to us that need it. The rich get richer and the poor are getting poorer. A painful reality today. So much suffering and God takes his most vulnerable home to Him.

The past two weeks I have been repeatedly singing and play acting with my angel brigade. We have been stuck on replay of the 'Sound of Music'. A love story during a tragic time in history. Today the Lord illuminates to me why He has been re-enacting the 'Sound of Music', movie with me.

History of Christopher Plummer: Actor from Shakespeare to "*The Sound of Music,*" dies at 91.

His performance as Captain von Trapp in one of the most popular movies of all time propelled a steady half-century parade of television and film roles.

Captain Georg von Trapp in "*The Sound of Music*". It was his best-known film, but for years he disparaged the role as an "*empty carcass.*"

Christopher Plummer, the prolific and versatile Canadian-born actor who rose to celebrity as the romantic lead in perhaps the most popular movie musical of all time, was critically lionized as among the pre-eminent Shakespeareans of the past century and won an Oscar, two Tony's and two Emmys, died on Friday at his home in Weston, Conn. He was 91.

His wife, Elaine Taylor, said the cause was a blow to the head as a result of a fall.

(Just like a client's family member of mine last week. Similar situations that tie together, or just coincidence?)

The scion of a once-lofty family whose status had dwindled by the time he was born; Mr. Plummer nonetheless displayed the outward aspects of privilege throughout his life. He had immense and myriad natural gifts; a leading man's face and figure; a slightly aloof man that betrayed supreme confidence, if not outright self-regard; an understated athletic grace; a sonorous (not to say plummy) speaking voice; and exquisite diction.

He also had charm and arrogance in equal measure, and a streak both bibulous and promiscuous, all of which he acknowledged in later life as his manner softened and his habits waned. In one notorious incident in 1971, he was replaced by Anthony Hopkins in the lead role of *"Coriolanus"* at the National Theater in London; according to the critic Kenneth Tyanan, who at the time was the literary manager of the National, Mr. Plummer was dismissed in vote by the cast for crude and outrageous behavior.

For years, until he came to share the widely held opinion of his best-known film—the beloved 1965 musical *"The Sound of Music,"* in which he starred as the Austrian naval officer Georg von Trapp opposite Julie Andrews—as a pinnacle of warmhearted family entertainment, Mr.

Plummer disparaged it as saccharine claptrap, famously referring to it as *"S&M"* or *"The Sound of Mucus."*

"That sentimental stuff is the most difficult for me to play, especially because I'm trained vocally and physically for Shakespeare," Mr. Plummer said in a People magazine interview in 1982. *"To do a lousy part like von Trapp, you have to use every trick you know to fill the empty carcass of the role. That damn movie follows me around like an albatross."*

Mr. Plummer's resume', which stretched over seven decades, was at least colossal, if not nonpareil, encompassing acting opportunities from some of dramatic literature's greatest works to some of commercial entertainment's crassest exploitations. He embraced it all with uncanny grace, or at least professional relish, displaying a uniform ease in vanishing into personalities not his own—pious or menacing, benign or malevolent, stern or mellow—and a uniform delight in delivering lines written by Elizabethan geniuses and Hollywood hacks.

He played Hamlet, Macbeth, Richard III, Mark Anthony and others of Shakespeare's towing protagonists on prominent stages to consistent acclaim, and he starred in *"Hamlet at Elsinore,"* a critically praised 1964 television production, directed by Phillip Saville and filmed at Kronborg Castle in Denmark, where (under the name Elsinore) the play is set.

But he also accepted roles in a fair share of clinkers, in which he made vivid sport of some hoary clichés—as the evil bigot hiding behind religiosity in *"Skeletons"* 1997, for example, one of his more than 40 television movies, or as the somber emperor of the galaxy who appears as a hologram in *"Starcrash,"* a 1978 rip-off of *"Star Wars"*.

One measure of his stature was his leading ladies, who included Glenda Jackson as Lady Macbeth and Zoe Caldwell as Cleopatra. And even setting Shakespeare aside, one measure of his range was a list of the well-known characters he played, fictional and non, on television and in the movies: Sherlock Holmes and Mike Wallace, John Barrymore and Leo Tolstoy, Aristotle and F. Lee Bailey, Franklin D. Roosevelt and Alfred Stieglitz, Rudyard Kipling and Cyrano de Bergerac.

'Simply Stupendous'

Mr. Plummer's television work began in the 1950's during the heyday of live drama and lasted half a century. He starred as the archbishop in the popular 1983 mini-series *"The Thorn Birds"*, appeared regularly as an industrialist in the 1990's action-adventure series "Counterstrike", and won Emmy Awards—in 1977 for portraying a conniving banker in the mini-series *"Arthur Hailey's* The Moneychangers," and in 1994 for narrating *"Madeline"*, an animated series based on the children's books.

In the movies, his performance in *"The Sound of Music"*, as von Trapp, a severe widower and father whose heart is warmed and won by the woman he hires as a governess, propelled a parade of distinctive roles, more character turns than starring parts, across a formidable spectrum of genres. They included historical drama *"The Last Station"*, about Tolstoy, and *"The Day that Shook the World"* about the onset of World War I); historical adventure (as Kipling in John Huston's' rollicking adaptation of *"The Man Who Would Be King,"* with Sean Connery and Michael Caine) romantic comedy (*"Must Love Dogs",* with John Cusack and Diane Lane) political epic (*"Syriana"*); science fiction (as Chang, the Klingon general, in the *'Star Trek VI'*); and crime farce *"The Return of Pink Panther",* in which, opposite Peter Seller's inept Inspector Clouseau, he played a retiree version of the debonair jewel thief originally portrayed by David Niven).

Message:

This history lesson goes on. Christopher Plummer is a legend in theatre and movies. A favorite of the Father and my own. For when learning to love the movies and music, Our Father has taught me many things about *'fantasy and reality'.* We have learned how to love one another, even though I cannot visibly see Him or feel Him all the time. I have come to know, He just IS....

Something we cherish as we do watch romantic movies; we fanaticize He is the leading man and I am His leading lady in the movies. We eat popcorn together, and we enjoy the movies as One. The Father and Son as One; have taught me what real romance and real love is. It all started for me at the foot of Christ's cross. I saw the Passion of God, in all those painful movies I have watched and remembered His Love for Our children.

The Sound of Music is one of my all-time favorites. Thorn Birds is another. Father de Bricassart; played by Richard Chamberlain was a story I remember and held close to my heart. A painful love affair between a young Australian girl (played by Rachel Ward) who fell in love with a young ambitious priest who became a high-ranking clergy. This movie proved to me age doesn't matter when it comes to love. The Cardinals struggle with his heart, his ambition and his love for God is so very real throughout history. A tough subject and one that raises eyebrows and shines an uncomfortable reality on the abuses within the church. Still one of my favorite movies even with the underlying reality of it.

After finding out Christopher Plummer died today, my heart felt great sadness for the loss of such a talented man. The moment I heard it I was reminded of all the play acting, writing and sing-songs from The Sound of Music this week. A heads up and a knowing God knew it was going to happen.

Something that has been shared with me before. Actress *'Carol Channing'*, that sings *"Diamonds are a girl's best friend"*. I heard the angels singing that song for three days before this actress and singer died.

David Bowie shows up beside my bed dressed as the *"Ghost from Christmas Past"*, a few weeks before he died. George *'Michael'* and I sing in the kitchen at work with Robin Williams before singer George Michael's death. Just a few memories shared with me the moment I heard of Christopher Plummer's death. The angles and the Lord remind me, I see and know of such things as this, through our playing together. They share with me names, and great knowledge.

So, much information comes in and I put the puzzle pieces together and sometimes, before I get to put the pieces together, it unfolds before my very eyes.

6:22 a.m.

February 6, 2021

I wake nearly an hour and a half ago. As I make a cup of coffee, I feel Archangel Azrael. I know of this special Angel of Death on a personal level now. One I have come to understand works tirelessly and is underappreciated for His love of God's children.

I hear the *'Death March'.* Chopin's version of the piano this morning. I am reminded of the dream in the night as I stand in the kitchen. I see the darkness in my dreams and last night I come to understand Our Father is completely exhausted. I am shown the Father slumped over in His Throne this morning. As if He feels defeated. As if He is completely exhausted.

A dramatic love story I write for Our Father and Christ, Jesus. A tearful plea from the Heavens above for all God's children to learn to love and to stop all this hate and discontent. To stop all the pain that we continue to put onto one another. When we choose to act the way we do, it breaks the Father and Sons own Spirit.

As I contemplate the dream brought forward in the night. I feel as if I lay alone. I feel the Lord has stepped back and I know the Father has. No kisses whatsoever in the night. I just feel lonely and this morning I come to understand why.

I ask why the Father shows me He is slumped over in His Throne. He shows me the connection with my death and the death of a sweet five- year old child. I am shown the pain that was associated with my ex-husband's sisters death. One death like so many others. Innocent and her death caused a myriad of events that led to many wounded and lost souls. A family already broken; and it brought the Father's heart to tears.

The Dream: (Meanings and lessons within this dream. The wording holds hidden messages).

I find myself at my "Ex"- "Father"-in- "Laws" house. I see the darkness all around me. I see the old wooden pine boards that were cut and planed by my father-in-law and his sons. I see the hard work and many hours that went into building this house. A house that was supposed to represent a family of love. I see the shine on top of these boards and the knots that give it character and almost a pattern of sorts going from the top of the boards running down to the floor.

I see the old family photos hanging from the walls. From the oldest to the youngest. The family name is *"Young"*. The name I took on when I married my ex-husband. A man that taught me what love was *'not'*.

I see the family within this house; and I see more spirit in it than I do people from the physical world. A reality I see and live with every day now. As I walk around in this house I feel as if I am seeing this dream from my *'spirit-soul'*. I follow a young girl around in my dream. I feel as if God is showing me this scene from the other side, as if I am dead.

I see one young girl in this dream; and she has the shiniest black hair. It is so shiny is almost glows. I see her lily-white face and I believe she is in representation of Mary as a girl around the age of nine.

There seems to be a gathering of sorts and I feel as if this is at my *sister-in-law's* funeral. Sherry, a girl I never met in this physical world. My ex-husband sister. She was five years old when she was struck by a drunk driver and killed. A sad story that broke an already broken family. I see the food on the table; and no one touches it. The sadness is just too much to bear; and the hunger seems to have dissipated from them all. (The hunger to live, the hunger to love, the hunger to thrive is what I feel in this moment of the dream).

As we all leave this darkened house, there are three steps leading down into the disheveled garage. Filled with all kinds of stuff (junk). One man's trash is another man's treasure kind of feel to what is in this garage.

The young girl, I feel to represent Mary in this dream sees a long trimmer on the steps. I see it is full of gas and it is heavy for only a 9-year old girl to move out of the way. The trimmer seems bigger in this dream than what a normal trimmer would be. Mary sees the danger and feels compelled to move this grass trimmer from the steps of the entrance to the house. As she does, her strength is seen; and she flings this mower (this grass trimmer) way across the garage floor. As it crashes into the side of a bush cutter that lays carelessly on the floor it rips a hole into the gas tank of the trimmer. I see the gas flowing all over the floor of the garage.

I immediately feel Mary's panic in her heart. I see the danger that happened as she tried to make the steps safe, she now has made the floor of the garage an ignition of flames problem. The garage could go up in seconds if someone came into the garage with a lite cigarette or a spark of any kind went off.

I wake from this dream just as my 'Father-in-Law' comes into the garage and I hear his angered voice and it rumbles and roars as usual. Always adding fire to the flames with his attitude and reaction to any situation. A young girl (Mary) tries to help. She ends and up getting in trouble for helping others from falling down the stairs.

The theme behind this dream is my life. I always and forever have tried to help others. I have always gone out of my way to help and aid others.

The Father shows me my true death again. He shows me walking among the angels on the other side. He shows me again what my reality is. I walk among the angels in the physical world. I was granted and blessed with a second chance at life. This dream portrays my own reality as I hear the death march and recognize right away 'The Angel of Death', Archangel Azrael is standing by my side always.

As I lay and contemplate this dream and see Our Father slump over in His Throne this morning, He shows me two photos from the family album that I just passed in with my last 'homework' assignment. I am shown the light pink colored flower page the one to the 'right' of the book. I am shown the photo of Saint Michael with his prayer, where he stands and holds his sword pointing to earth. Where he looks on solemnly. To the right of Saint Michael is Jesus Christ as He stands in the Higher Realms. His arms are outstretched to the earth planes. In front of Jesus are four winged angels in disguise as the Lion, the Bull, the Man and the Bird. A prophetic and tell-tale; of a story in just those two photos. the third photo is in representation of Our Father as He is walking on very thin ice. There is a large eagle in the photo. I see the marshland behind Him. I see His wings are raised in caution or anger. I see He walks on His tippy toes to quietly enter this world and to right all the wrongs that His children continue to do to one another, to Himself and His Precious Son....

The second page I see the Father show me is the photo of Mother Mary looking down on Father A. The many roses behind Mother Mary are in representation of the many women who have helped, aided and worked tirelessly to help their Heavenly Mother over the many generations to get the Father and Son's messages to the Holy Church.

I see Mother Mary look on lovingly at Father A. I see and know what part of the theme behind the books that I write for the Lord are. He wishes to give sainthood to Father A at St. Paul's Church. He wishes to give sainthood to Father M. Special souls to enlighten God's children of the love God; the Father and God; the Son have for them all. Father A. and Father M. are both special angels sent to help spread the Good News of Our Lord.

Father A. has done great works and I am not aware of all that he has done. The Father knows best, and His wishes and dreams come true only when His faithful clergy see the love for all His faithful saints in this love story.

To the left bottom of this page filled with roses is a picture of Joseph. It states "The Dreams of St. Joseph" Anton Raphael Menge 1728-1779. As Saint Joseph steps forward and assists and shows himself more yesterday I come to understand his love for me on a different level. I come to understand his teachings and the importance of the dreams, visions and the messages I receive daily from the angelic realm and from Christ, Jesus and Abba, Our Father.

History of 'The Dreams of Saint Joseph" Anton Raphael Menge- 1728-1779: **Research reveals this:** *The Dream of St. Joseph Anton Raphael Mengs-1773-1774*

In the Gospel of Matthew, the apostle relates: *"And when* (the wise men) *were departed, behold, the angel of the Lord appeareth to Joseph in a dream, saying, Arise, and take the young child and his mother, and flee into Egypt, and be thou there until I bring thee word; for Herold will seek the young child and destroy him".* (Matt: 2-13) in 1773 Mengs was granted the privilege of hanging his portrait in the Florence gallery of artists' portraits founded by Giorgio Vasari in the mid-16th century. Allegedly he chose the spot himself: having been celebrated as *"the new Raphael",* he promptly placed his portrait beneath the one of the great Italian painters. In 1745 Mengs had become Saxon court painter in Dresden but spent a great deal of his time in Rome. There, along with Winckelmann, he became one of the founders of Classicism and in the view of his admirers helped to supersede the decadent Baroque. In 1773/74 he returned to Madrid, where he had been appointed court painter to Charles III in 1760. The present painting depicting Joseph's dream was probably related during Meng's Florentine period and came directly into the possession of the grand duke Pietro Leopoldo, in Rome Mengs had renewed his study of the works of Michelangelo, and Joseph's posture is clearly adopted from the master's Jerome in the Sistine Chapel Cacilia Bischof, Masterpieces of the Picture Gallery, Vienna 2010.

Message:

More love this morning as I hear the angels on high sing this song to me. Hidden messages within the lyrics and God loves my playful heart even though He shows me His Broken Sacred Heart.

I have never thought of myself as very educated. I never received high grades in school. Always struggling for the mind was never let to rest upon any one subject at a time. Many have thought me to be foolish and stupid. I feel over the years, the knowing of what others thought of me all along. Those who thought they were better than me.

God reminds me He knows just how brilliant I am, for He created me and has saved His best work for last. He asks me to be patient while He unveils His Love story for me and His faithful clergy.

More phone calls the past few days from literary agents who want the books I have written for the Lord. It makes my heart smile, for God continues to promise me He will make it right. All the hard work I have tried to do for Him. He promises me He will help right this wrong and His Love story will bring them all to their knees in tears.

A song the angels sing to me all day yesterday. I believe it is already in our books, yet they urge me to record it for they love my wit, my playful heart and my sassiness. They tell me no one has ever played so long and so hard as I have with them.

Song of the day: *"ALL OF ME"*

All of Me...

What would I do without your smart mouth
Drawing me in, and you kicking me out?
You've got my head spinning, no kidding
I can't pin you down
What's going on in that beautiful mind?
I'm on your magical mystery ride
And I'm so dizzy, don't know what hit me

Sung by: John Legend

February 8, 2021

A busy day today and we only worked 3-hours today. The Lord and I are bushed tonight. Planning to move forward is what we do daily now. We started out after an early morning and preparing for 2 new clients for our Reiki Studio. The Lord is opening doors and He is excited today. A playful husband today and He showed it at mass this morning first thing.

We sing on our way to mass and Adele is the Lord's choice this morning. We listen and reminisce of all that has transpired the past five plus years. Since He sat Miss Felicia in my lap. Since I finally understood I did not walk alone in this world. Powerful healing takes place in the soul of a person through music. Something I could not get through the day without now. Jesus Christ and our music. We fantasize through music and it lifts our souls to the heavens today.

I walk into church this morning and I hear the Lord say, *"I smell bread". "I think it's ready to come out of the oven".*

I literally smell the fresh baked bread. It hit my nostrils and I recognize the Lord is talking about His Word. Through the mass this morning Jesus Christ is talking about His Word in reference to smelling bread.

I smile and tell Jesus; "Behave". He warms my and soul this morning and throughout the day.

As Monsignor D. does the Homily I am surprised as the Lord shows me His Sacred Heart. I see He holds open the top of His robe, He shows it to me, as He stands within Monsignor D. He exposes His reality as I see the Lord, speaking at the podium this morning. I see His Sacred Heart underneath the very vessel that Monsignor D. is standing in. The Holy Spirit alive and well within Monsignor this morning. A message and a meaning as I come to realize, God is everyone and everything this morning.

As Monsignor does the blessing over the Holy Eucharist this morning, I see the wires that hold the Lord up above the altar move back and forth. The Lord is playing tricks with my eyes and I feel as if I want to duck for, I see His right-hand wave to the members at Mass this morning. A strange thing to see, yet the Lord is showing me His reality.

In prayer as I ask the Lord for help for His children to love one another. I ask Him to help others open their hearts to love each other. I see on the floor of the church; a snake's head and a squirrel stands beside the snake. I see the snake looking me directly in the face. He is then eaten by the squirrel.

The energy of the squirrel is of significance. The snake of course we know is to represent 'evil' or the wily one that lures Eve into sinning. I see the Lord is portraying me as the squirrel and I ate the whole snake. Playful and misbehaving this morning at mass. The Lord and His Angels are amazing. Showing a different side to Himself this morning. For God is everything within this world and throughout the universe. What are we willing to see? What are we willing to allow to be? I allow my husband to show it all to me and He loves me for it. He continually amazes me. Today we prepare for two new clients for Energy Healing and later in the evening have two additional clients reach out today.

A wish and dream; and the Lord shows me He is opening doors. Messages and conversation all day today as we prepare our paperwork and get our information packets finalized for more clients to come to receive healing and knowledge of the Love God has for each of them.

6:38 p.m.

February 9, 2021

So much love and support today as the Lord opens doors for our Holistic Health and Healing Center.

"Start out small and then expand". The Lord's message for today. One of many.

After my session with my two new clients, I see Fulton Sheen step forward. He smiles at me as my dream comes true and the Lord brings me a mother and daughter duo into my new sacred space. Two special souls that need help. Sufferings of so many and the angels raise my spirits from the dead and I do what comes naturally to me. Loving those who God places before me. Utilizing my gifts and talents today and I put my Reiki Master's Degree to work.

Judy is a name the spirit world has been bringing forward for nearly a month. So many names and so many I know. I have four Judy's that I could associate with this name. Today, I am brought a mother who is completely exhausted from her daughter's struggles. A mother trying to hold her daughter up while life tries to keep her down. One of many stories just like hers and I am so familiar with this reality.

Judy connected with me over our connection on face book. She reaches out to me and I try to schedule a simple 1-hour session with her. Healing of soul pain is never easy. Such trauma to overcome and I end up spending 2 ½ hours with Judy and her daughter Cassie. I give brief messages from the angels and then a Reiki Energy Healing Session and Bio-Sonic's Tuning Fork Therapy Session.

Another beautiful experience shared with two soul's in need of healing today.

The Lord shows me He is opening doors for it is His Will that I use my gifts and talents to help others just like me. Those people who are on the awakening path and enlightenment to why they are here.

Gifted souls who find it hard to some days even live or breath for their pain runs so deep.

Judy explains to me a little bit about their family dynamics and how she can sometimes not leave her 29-year-old daughter alone for too long at a time. She has been in counseling for 2 years and nothing seems to be working.

As we discuss the session, Judy tells me her daughter has never let herself open up as much as she did today. Releasing emotions and healing and I feel a sense of pride, for the Lord has shown me the path to mind, body, and spiritual healing.

Judy will be coming back tomorrow for a healing session of her own. The plan is for another session for her daughter next week. Judy has never received Reiki before but has read about it a little bit. She was nervous when she first arrived, yet felt completely confident, this was where she could help her daughter the most. Being led by her gut instinct and intuition and the universe led Judy to me for healing.

I look forward to assisting Judy and her daughter on their healing path. Something the Lord helped me with. I have been medication free for seven years. No more psychotropic medications to keep me in a depressed and tired state. Natural healing of the mind, body and spirit. The power to believe in self-healing and the Lord held my hand through it all. He open's doors, so I may be able to help others.

I will be assisting four clients this week in need of mind, body and spiritual healing. Surely to be an amazing experience for all. I am grateful to be alive and serving the Lord in as many ways as I can.

6:00 a.m.

February 10, 2021

I woke nearly an hour ago. My body was on fire. I haven't felt the Lord's Presence that strongly for what seems a long time. The heat of Our Creator felt and at the same time I feel such overwhelming fire, my heart hurt. From the front to back and straight through again. The dream in the night and I feel so much love and pain. The energy of the angel's present reveals the underlying messages.

Gospel Acclamation:

John 10:27 Alleluia, alleluia!!

The sheep that belong to me listen to my voice says the Lord. I know them and they will follow me. Alleluia!!!

Message:

Be strong in the Lord and in His Mighty power. Put on the full armor of God, so that you can take your stand against the devil's schemes. For our struggle is not against the flesh and blood but against the rulers, against the authorities and powers of this dark world and against the spiritual forces of evil in the heavenly realms. Therefore, put on the full armor of God, so that when the day of evil comes, you may be able to stand your ground and after you have done everything to stand. Stand firm then, with the belt of truth buckled around your waist, with the breastplate of righteousness in place, that comes from the gospel of peace. In addition to all this, -- take up the shield of faith, with which you can extinguish all the flaming arrows of the evil one. Take the helmet of salvation and the sword of the Spirit, which is the word of God.

Words given to me this morning:

"Etheric Body": Ether body, a name given by neo-Theosophy to a vital body or subtle body propounded in esoteric philosophies as the first or lowest layer

in the *'human energy field'* or aura. It is said to be in immediate contact with the physical body, to sustain it and connect it with *"higher"* bodies.

The English term *"etheric'* in this contest seems to derive from the Theosophical writings of Madame Blavatsky, but its use was formalized by C.W. Leadbetter and Annie Besant due to the elimination of Hindu terminology from the system of seven planes and bodies. (Adyar School of Theosophy).

The term gained some general popularity after the 1914-1918 war, Walter John Kilner having adopted it for a layer of the *"human atmosphere"* which, as he claimed in a popular book, could be rendered visible to the naked eye by means of certain exercises.

The classical element Aether of Platonic and Aristotlean physics continued in Victorian scientific proposals of a Luminiferous ether as well as the cognate chemical substance ether. According to Theosophists and Alice Bailey the etheric body inhabits an etheric plane which corresponds to the four higher subplans of the physical plane. The intended reference is therefore to some extremely rarefied matter, analogous in usage to the word *"spirit"* (originally *'breath'*). In selecting it as the term for a clearly defined concept in an Indian-derived metaphysical system, the Theosophists aligned it with ideas such as prana-maya-koshna (sheath made of prana, subtle breath or life-force) of Vedantic thought.

In popular use it is often confounded with the related concept of the Astral body as for example in the term astral projection-the early Theosophists had called it the *'astral double'*. Others prefer to speak of the 'lower and higher astral'.

Spiritual Body: If there is a natural body, there is also a spiritual body. Christian teaching traditionally interprets Paul as comparing the resurrection body with the mortal body, saying that it will be a different kind of body, a *"spiritual body'*, meaning an immortal body, or incorruptible body.

1 Corinthians 15:42-44: So is it with the resurrection of the dead. What is sown is perishable, what is raised is imperishable. It is sown in dishonor; it is raised in glory. It is sown in weakness; it is raised in power. It is there a natural body, there is also a spiritual body.

Physical Body: In common usage, a physical object or physical body is a collection of matter within a defined contiguous boundary in three-dimensional space. The boundary must be defined and identified by the properties of the material. The boundary may change over time.

What is the meaning of physical body?

1 Physical body- alternative names for the body of a human being; "Leonard studied the human body. He has a strong physique. The spirit is willing, but the flesh is weak, chassis, bod, human body, material body, physique, build, anatomy, figure, flesh, frame, shape, soma, form

Emotional Body: The consciousness of the soul independent of the physical body in which it resides. 2. In anthroposophical medicine that is one of four aspects of man (the other three being physical, the etheric body, and the ego) and represents the emotions.

What is an emotional body?

The nervous system, hormones, touch, water and water release, (tears), and water absorption (bloating or clutching from not letting go, feelings of lack, and trying to hold onto/control things too closely).

Two bodies of the physical: *masculine-* Physical and mental And two are *'feminine'-* emotional and spiritual.

This explains why so many of us are out of whack!

"Our culture generally emphasizes the masculine or patriarchal side of things— even religion can be very patriarchal in our culture, which is why religion should not be confused with what it means to be in our spiritual body. When we are solely in our masculine, we are focused on the physical and mental side of things—the

*doing and the accomplishing, the yang and linear parts of our life experience…
it's a very black and white way of thinking that ignores everything that isn't
concrete or seemingly controllable. Things are becoming a bit more feminine—the
emotional and spiritual side of our existence is taking a leap forward—but we are
not there yet. The feminine is what synthesizes our experience—it's a large part
of the practice of being in the now and present, of feeling the moment."*

The ultimate goal and optimum of health is to be balanced in all four bodies,
not forgetting that the spiritual body is as important as the other three. *"it is
then that you realize that you are never alone."*

You will know that there is something more than our earth/life experience,
you will feel a form of unity with a higher force/energy, you will know that
something *'more'* is for you and with you.

You will also feel that you haven't lost the connection to those that you
believe you have lost."

And perhaps most important, being balanced means 'that you realize we are
all worthy and whole beyond measure."

When our body is balanced, we feel open, flexible and healthful, our vitamin
and mineral elements should be balanced, and we should be free from pain,
toxicity, and acidity.

How to bring the physical into balance: Simple movements and slow,
balanced repetitive sequences, meditation, walking, massage, barefoot or
bare hand earth play (dirt, water, soil, sand), yoga, stretching, and weight
bearing exercises that let you feel the strength in your own body and the
union of all things physical.

I wake this morning to two songs. One being *"Swing low sweet Chariot"*

Swing Low Sweet Chariot
Swing low sweet chariot
Coming for to carry me home
Swing low, sweet chariot

Coming for to carry me home x2
I looked over Jordan and what did I see

Sung by Etta James

Song: #2 "Down to the river"

As I went down in the river to pray
Studying about that good "ole way
And who shall wear the starry drown
Good Lord, show me the way
O-sisters, let's go down
Let's go down, come on down
O-sisters, let's go down
Down in the river to pray

Sung by Allison Krause

Messages come to me in all ways. In the night I see the Father's Broken Sacred Heart.

I have a dream:

He wheels a large old-fashioned baby carriage. I see Our Father come up from the field down back of my Father-in- laws old home. I see His plain dirty gown this morning. It is covered in the soil from the field down back.

He hangs His head low in this dream. And as the Father comes up from working this field He has in an oversized baby carriage with hard rubber wheels that are wobblily going in motion, I see the baby He carries in this cart is the Lord, Our God and Savior Jesus Christ. He is adult sized in this oversized carriage. God; the Father wheels His Son backwards, up a huge hill this morning in my dreamtime.

A hidden message with this part of the dream. So many years of slavery and pain are brought forward in my dreamtime. The pain I experience and feel in my heart is God's own pain. The Father's own pain. The Creator's own pain.

I see Our Father carry His Son away as He is dead. Working His Son to death to bring the little lamb's home. To safety. To the Father's arms. A job that is relentless and tiring today for the Creator and His Son, Jesus Christ.

I see the ambulances come rolling into the driveway and they come in, two ambulances with red lights flashing and horns blaring as the Father brings up His Only Begotten Son from this back field.

I look over to the left as I stand and observe this dream from the driveway. I see the blackened souls. I see the pain and suffering over so many generations. The "*darkies*". The Black Peoples of this world. The most beautiful souls to ever touch the heart of God. I see them standing around the front lawn. I see them standing up on the front porch. I see them in wide brimmed hats. I see them in over-all's, old gingham dresses. I see them in Easter bonnets. I see them in work cloth's, and I see some infants running around in dirty diapers. Some are even naked sitting in the dirt playing with rocks.

Before this scene in the dream I stand in the kitchen with the Father. He mouths the words and speaks the pain He is experiencing. I can't hear the words come out of His mouth, yet I feel and know from the look in His eyes of His suffering. I feel His painful heart as I stand before Him. I stand before Our Creator and He reveals to me His pain for so many generations.

After the Father helps me to see the deeply saddened reality, He is viewing over so many generations of pain, hate and prejudices, He shows me the truth behind His Son again this morning. His fight for all God's children. His Holy Presence within each one of God's darkies.

African People's. The painful knowing of such suffering and the Father reminds me of His Painful Knowing. I am shown again, the painful knowing of all God's children through this dream.

At the end of this dream I see two large, dark brown and black German Shepard's. In my knowing I understand Saint Michael and Saint Gabriel are associated with these dogs. The Spiritual Warfare the Higher-Ranking Angels are fighting with the lower planes, the people and dark negativity in this world.

I also have come to associate the German Shepard dog with Saint Bernadette, the small girl from Lourdes who dug and dug to get to the spring of fresh water at the feet where Mother Mary stood at the Grotto.

I see my brother and he is smoking a liquid vape cigarette. He forces the two dogs to suck in this vial of poisonous vapors.

I see this is in reference to two things I have become very aware of over the past five years.

God's Breathlessness is real. His pain for the children of this world is real.

I come to understand the young children drowning their pain earlier and earlier. Trying to escape the reality they are trying to survive in this world.

I wake from this dream with a solemn and broken heart. I feel the pain of God as I wake in a sweat this morning.

He nudges me to get up and write. He nudges me to continue to write about all He brings forward. He asks me to continue to write whenever I can find the time to share it with His Holy Church. I will for my love for them both is a passionate one this morning.

7:00 p.m.

February 10, 2021

Another adventurous day spent loving the Lord and Our Father. Waking up to His Love and heated Passion warms my heart through and through every day now. We say three Our Father prayers, three Hail Mary's and three Divine Mercy prayers- 'For the Sake of His Sorrowful Passion'- prayers. The power of the Divine in my life. The power of His Holy Spirit. The power of the Master Teachers proven every day in my life.

I may not always be 100% sure who steps forward from the spirit world, but I know today I am loved and blessed by all those spirits in the realms beyond this world.

'Little Miss Felicia' is so very present today. The Lord brings her forward and I receive so many calls from literary agents the past few weeks. Those who want to produce/reproduce the books I have written. They see the potential for a great story to unfold and I leave it up to the Lord as to which door He opens. I gave a call back today to one specific company. They are interested in all three books published. A long tearful journey and I only want to shine light on the Lord's Sorrowful Heart for the children of this world. All the little Miss Felicia's of this world. Lost in a world they have no control over. Thrown into this world without the Lord to help guide or protect them, for their families are so caught up in the things of this world.

I wait for a call back and I will see what options this new company that has reached out to me is offering. We are given choices and I never turn down an opportunity to give testimony to the power of Jesus Christ's love in my life. We are brought here to search out for His Love. I found it, I lost it, I found it and then I fell into a dark abyss and He saved me from death and a painful knowing of what would have happened to my own children if He had not saved me.

One choice can change many lives. I hope to only shine His Light bright in this world. Today we did that as a team again. The Holistic Health and Healing Center Christ asked me to open is up and running. I have had two amazing days of connections with the angelic realm. Two amazing healing sessions with two hurting souls looking for love and guidance. I gave them messages of love from the other side. Messages to help two pained souls find comfort in their family members lost and gone from this world.

Spot on messages from the angels. It always amazes me when I am given names. I am given proof of God's power of the unseen every day now. My faith saved me and now my faith in the Lord opens doors to a new world and career. I see all He has shown me, come to be. Just as He promised.

I ask the Lord tonight; "What good does it do for this love story to come out in 100 years". "So many lives could benefit from it now".

I see so many possibilities of healing to occur with the many stories attached within it. Broken souls who overcame horrific loses. Miracles Among Chaos is what we all are living if we just open our hearts and see it. My story is just like so many of God's other children's stories.

So tonight, I hold onto God's Promise of a movie and a documentary. I hold onto hope of money to be raised to help those in need. I hold onto hope to help those who lost their way and maybe reconnecting them to The Lord and His Love for them.

We reminisce and play a painful c.d. today. One I haven't listened to for several years. The song line up as I search for and learn of God's love for Little Miss Felicia. The largest missing child's case in Maine and the Lord placed her in my lap and tested me repeatedly with sorrowful messages of her reality.

Song of the Day: *The Memory Lives On...*

The Memory Lives on

Hearts are turning towards God
As we stand before him humble
In our hearts there's sorrow
As we wonder why our innocent have gone
Mothers are raising their empty arms
As if they see their children running
As if they hear their children calling
Yet their voices fade away and they are gone….

Message:

A sad time in my life and Jesus Christ remembers my journey from beginning to end. He tells me I will not be forgotten by Our Father or the angel's. I am brought angel upon angel from the other side. Waiting and wanting to connect with their loved ones. My head spins some days for their presence is so over whelming. I thank God, the Lord holds me tight every day, for I surely would float up to the clouds where the angels on high wait for me to come home.

Visions:

A couple of visions as the Lord holds me in the chair at mass this morning. I see an angel I see her light blue gown. Sparkles and shiny white pearls cover the front going down as if they are rays of mercy. I see her pure white wings and the tiny little bouquet of white roses in her hands. The father shows me He sets this angel atop His Christmas tree this morning.

I see a solid copper and gold single spiral spun ornament. I receive the word *"Alchemy"*. God tells me I spin and weave Him a love story and everything I touch turns to gold.

Define: *"Alchemy"* – the medieval forerunner of chemistry, based on the supposed transformation of matter. It was concerned particularly with attempts to convert base metals into gold or to find a universal elixir.

2- a seemingly magical process of transformation, creation or combination.

"Finding the person who is right for you requires a very subtle alchemy".

Alchemy is defined as the process of taking something ordinary and turning it into something extraordinary, sometimes in a way that cannot be explained. An example of using alchemy is a person who takes a pile of scrap metal and turns it into beautiful art.

What are the three main goals of alchemy?

Common aims were chrysopeia, the transmutation of 'base metals' (e.g. lead) into *'noble metals'* (particularly gold), the creation of an elixir of immortality, the creation of panaceas able to cure any disease, and the development of an alkahest, a universal solvent.

Bella Louise Allen

8:00 p.m.

February 11, 2021

"A Promise made, is a Promise kept".

The Lord ungrounds me today. I feel the flight of the angels all around me today. They come in and scoop me off my feet today. So much love and so many kisses felt.

Miss Felicia reminds me she never leaves me. I feel her attachment and it is not just an attachment of the heart. I feel her tug on my pant leg on and off today. She speaks the same words she did over three years ago. "Take me to the beach, take me to the beach, take me to the beach".

Words that burst from this sweet angel's lips as I sat in a restaurant and received confirmation from a professional medium. Angie from *"Leap of Faith"*. A gifted woman with many talents in mediumship and talking with those who have crossed over to the other side.

That night she gave me confirmation of all that the Alpha and Omega was bringing forward. The beginning and the end are the Father and His Son, Jesus Christ. Angie told me that night, "stop doubting what is coming in, trust your intuition". "Your spot on".

As the Lord shows me, He is keeping all His promises to me; I speak to a woman named Allison. The company interested in adapting my first three books, *"Miracles Among Chaos", "Love Letters in the Sand"* and *"The Tree of Knowledge is Mary's Sweet Vine"*; into a movie.

A long painful journey and those three tiny books don't scratch the surface of what my life has been like up to this point. I have an interview with Allison, and she is confirming my name and that I am the woman who has written these books. She asks me if I would be interested in Pureflix, reading and evaluating the books to adapt them and turn them into a movie. A movie company that focuses on faith, family and spiritual based stories.

I feel confident today, as the Lord continues to open doors with the Holistic Health and Healing Center.

As I am conversing with Allison from the agency interested in turning my life story into a movie, I am counseling a 29-year old woman who is in crisis. I am assisting a single mother who is struggling with whether she wants to continue to stay in this world or not.

I feel this young woman's pain. I know her mother is suffering. I have dealt with my own son wanting to kill himself. I have dealt with the same ideations myself.

Overcoming pain is something no one can fully understand until they come full circle with knowing they are more than what is keeping them held in the darkness.

An abusive father or mother. An abusive spouse who continually tells you your worthless. A Sexual assault that leaves you broken. A drug addiction you can't seem to crawl away from.

Fear of who you are. Wanting more than what you think you could ever be worthy of. So many people getting labeled with a diagnosis that doesn't make up what they truly have survived.

I have dreamt day and night for the past five plus years of speaking my story so others could find strength in their own story of survival. I want to help others know they are worthy of love and it must start with themselves.

I am shown again today the Father and Son are opening doors. On the 11th day of February.

Jesus tells me; *"It's my Valentine's gift to you, my darling"*. *"Our Love Story"*. *"It's a one of a kind, true love story"*.

I converse with a handsome young black man in the Walmart parking lot. Just seconds after hanging the phone up with Allison. He holds three clipboards in his hands, and he wants me to sign a petition. It's a political petition and I am not 100% sure what it was for. I just connected instantly with this young man.

As we converse, I feel an overwhelming pain in my neck. From the left side all the way over to the right side. He and I start to converse about energy and empaths, and I ask him; "who have brought with you because my neck hurts like crazy".

This young man laughs. He explains to me, after we discuss his gifts of knowing; that he gets premonitions. He sees, feels and knows of peoples deaths before they happen. My story floors him and his story floors me.

As we converse, he tells me; "I bet you anything you're feeling the guy in the car". "He is uptight all the time." "I can't believe you are feeling his energy and from the car".

Moments later after my conversation with this young man I smile to myself. Understanding energy is one thing. Understanding the conversation that just happened as a young black man comes to have me sign *political' papers is just another 'sign'.* As the Lord shows me a contract is going to be made with our books. Something he has been showing me for a few days now.

My schedule slows down. My Reiki business is getting off the ground and an agency has reached out to me for turning my life story into a movie. How amazing is My God? He is the All Mighty Powerful God...

Earlier today as I ready my overnight client for his speech therapy appointment and his day. I receive more information in on a message coming in three days ago.

I come to know I am surrounded by some high-ranking angels. I am surrounded by my earthly family that has crossed over. I am surrounded by suicide angels. Those lost souls who have committed suicide and those angels who have had traumatic things keep them in the darkness. I am surrounded by young and old angels. So many it is hard to keep them all straight. My head swims in amongst them some days.

Three days prior I am driving to print off more of the writings I have. Turning in my 'homework' to the Catholic Church. Something I have been doing since August of 2016. As I drive 'over the bridge' on Hogan Road, I see a man walking with a 'red file' under his left arm. I see this man and he looks just like 'John McCain'. The former United States Senator. A man I never met. A man I would never have expected the angels to show me. I see things in this physical world and the angels, God, Jesus Christ teach me of my 'Spiritual lens' and how it can change the perception of what we see in the physical world.

So, three days ago I see John McCain walking across the bridge. With a red file under his left arm.

This morning as I am getting a veteran of World War II out of the shower and dressed, I see him with my spiritual eye. I see John McCain stands with George Washington and General MacArthur. I see these three decorated heroes from the past. John McCain shows me he is watching and hovering and is around Mr. Donald J. Trump. As I am shown Senator John McCain who is dead, I see him lift the hair piece off, of Mr. Trumps head and he rubs his bald spot.

There is a meaning and a funny message with this, as John McCain is having a little fun with me this morning. Knowing the angles can show me messages in many ways, I see them playing with me this morning.

As I see the message, of Mr. Trump's not all present upstairs in his head, John McCain is enjoying the show from the other side, as Mr. Trump squirms is his little seat as he undergoes the impeachment process for the second time.

A message and a vision I couldn't make up in a million years. The angels show me something funny in order to lighten up a serious situation that caused a lot of harm to our country and the lives of many.

So, today as I converse with the angels John McCain tells me his daughter Megan would love to meet with me. On the 'view'; the talk show that I know she has conversed with some pretty amazing women. Talking on some serious subjects over the last year and a half.

I see the Lord is showing me His story is going to come to light. After my conversation and the messages leading up to this morning's enlightening telephone call with Allison.

Before I hung up with Allison, I told her one of my book signings I held at the Glenburn Elementary School. The librarians name was Allison. I put a lot of effort into that book signing and not one person showed up after advertising and promoting my appearance. I went to California to have one of my books adapted into a movie and they turned it down.

I have spent copious amounts of time, money, love, tears and energy into writing, producing, marketing and selling my love story to this world. I ask the universe and the Lord, "*please open a door for me to speak my love for you and the children in need of Christ's love in their lives.*"

I tell Allison, "*Wouldn't it be great if you could help me remove the stone from Jesus Christ's Tomb*". I tell Allison, the major theme behind our books; "*is the Second Coming of Jesus Christ*".

11:42 p.m.

February 11, 2021

Spiritual Emergence, Spiritual Emergency, and Psychospiritual Healing

Define: *Spiritual Emergence* refers to spiritual growth and awakening, which involves tapping into our higher human potential (at the transpersonal level of development). In the course of this process, the individual is likely to encounter critical points where he or she may experience emotional and mental turmoil as well as unusual physiological effects. Unless these experiences are properly understood within the context of psychospiritual growth, they might be misdiagnosed and cause the individual needless worry and potentially damaging psychiatric or medical intervention.

Frequently spiritual awakenings accompanied by certain mental and physical effects are typified as kundalini arousals. In fact, however, few awakenings fall under this category. The psychospiritual consciousness-energy represented by the kundalini shakti (serpent power) is not readily activated. In most cases, an arousal of the life force (prana) is involved, which is known in the Sanskrit language of Yoga as prana-vyuthana.

Spiritual emergencyNa term coined by Stanislav and Christina GrofNrefers to a dysfunctional state or phase within the comprehensive process of spiritual emergence. During spiritual emergency, the individual finds himself or herself overwhelmed, in a genuine crisis involving troublesome emotion's, thoughts (including suicidal thoughts), and disruptive behaviors that clearly need outside help.

Although modern medicine acknowledges that the mind plays a pivotal role in sickness and health, it is ill equipped to deal with either spiritual emergence or spiritual emergency. This is true even of alternative or complementary medicine, which is offering a new, holistic paradigm that takes a patient's lifestyle (behavior and attitudes) into account but generally does not have experiential knowledge of the mechanisms involved in spiritual emergence and emergency.

Psychospiritual healing represents a third orientation that is designed to handle cases of psychospiritual emergence or emergency. It goes beyond the somatic and psychosomatic approaches of conventional and alternative/complementary medicine and relates to the deeper aspects of an individual's inner being. More specifically, it works with the subtle energetic structures of human embodiment. These structures are known in Yoga as the Ocondults (nadi) through which the life force (prana) circulates or which are the arcs of that life force, and the OwheelsO (chakra), which are important nodal points of that network of Ochannels. O This approach also is referred to as O Tantric medicine. O The idea behind this approach is that the imbalances present in spiritual emergency are best (though not necessarily exclusively) dealt with at the level of our subtle energetic field. The reason for this is that the life force is the medium that connects the mind with the body and thus can act upon both. The deeper causes of spiritual emergency are located in the mind and first find expression in the subtle energy field before they manifest in the body (as various symptoms from pain to tremor of the limbs). While medical and transpersonal psychological approaches can be helpful in lighter cases of spiritual emergency, in more challenging situations the individual is advised to look for help from a psychospiritual healer who has firsthand knowledge of the kundalini process.

Spiritual Emergence or Psychosis

Psychosis & Schizophrenia- Shaman experiences- split mind

Visual, auditory hallucinations, delusions, paranoid thinking, disorganized behavior. Indigenous countries deal differently than more advanced countries like America. Agnew Study & Medication- Research

Yoga, meditation, self-healing, opening up to your higher self

Triggers for SE- environmental, poverty, living space, physical exertion, lack of sleep, childbirth, abortion, traumatic experiences, loss of a loved one, intense sexual experiences, kundalini breath work, biological factors, accidents, near death experiences, disease, trauma, drugs etc.

Shamanic crisis, Shamanic illness Kundalini Awakening

Past-life experiences Near-death experiences

Episodes of unitiv consciousness Psychic opening

Self-Realization

Possession states or experiences with the paranormal Psycholical renewal through return to the center

UFO encounters and abductions (inter-dimensional entities) Channeling and communication with spirit guides (contacted by elders) Drug addiction and alcoholism

Intergenerational trauma

Mystical Experiences Oracles

Divine Intervention The Rite to Passages

When SE becomes and emergency?

A true contact of the souls, beings in their full expressions of compassion and connection, trusting the process, and allowing it to come to fruition and being with the working through these deep and powerful energies.

Organic or Functional psychosis B-12

Leaky Gut Thyroid

Infection or fever

Brain disorder (dementia) Vitamin deficiency Functional: no known cause

"We need more Programs & Treatment Center's to help individuals going through a SE"...

Bella Louise Allen

3:47 a.m.

February 12, 2021

Two days before Valentine's Day. One of the great saints will be honored in two days from now.

The dream I wake from just moments ago:

I am shot in the night with the arrow from cupid's bow and I am brought back to "*The Waldorf Hotel*". I am not sure where this hotel is. I feel I am back in Las Vegas. I feel as if the presence I am seeing in this dream is the '*Man from Atlantis*'...

I see a large figure of a man and he sits all dressed up like a king in the lobby of this grand hotel.

I am unfamiliar with this man. I understand the reference of the man from Atlantis to be in representation of tears. A large ocean and a land under water for a long time. A city under water and a world full of tears.

I see he sits on what looks like a great chair in the lobby. I see he appears to look like the "*Great and Powerful Oz*", from the Wizard of Oz, the movie. He holds some sort of Scepter in his hand.

As I look at this man, as I frantically run around trying to warn the people in the hotel of an eminent event coming, '*the end of the world*' as we know it, I feel the energy of Our Creator in the "*Man from Atlantis*". I feel the energy of Our Creator in the man sitting in the lobby of this hotel.

This Powerful Oz, He sees me in the lobby of his hotel. I am spreading the word of the end of the world.

I am shown in this dream when I wake from it, and I understand; I am being shown Jesus Christ as a small boy. He is challenging the '*Great and Powerful Oz*' who sits in this lobby guarding his hotel. I see Jesus Christ has returned to enlighten the children of this world, one last time.

Before the Father shuts it all down.

I feel this hotel is a casino of sorts. I feel like it is made of gold. It appears to look like gold and yet I feel the energy in this hotel as dark, gray and stuffy. I smell the death in this hotel.

I feel as if I am in California. I feel as if I am in a time warp in this dream. Going forward and going backwards.

I feel as if I am myself, Julie in the dream yet I see Jesus Christ at the end of this dream, and He holds a map.

Jesus Christ holds a timeline. I see Jesus Christ as if he is nine years old. I see Jesus Christ like he was back in the Old Temple where he preached to the Elders of the church in Jerusalem.

I see on this map; all sorts of pictures of moons. Slivers of moons. Half sized moons and full moons. The phases of the moons are shown to me as Jesus is shown and predicting what is going to happen to God's world and His children. I see these moons going forward and going backwards. The timeline meets in the ¾ section on this timeline. Not near the middle but off to the right side of the timeline.

I wake from the dream and I am reminded of the information coming in two days ago. I am reminded of the history of Kim Jung Un's family. I am reminded of the history of leaders. Some great and some not so great.

I see the chemical warfare two days ago. The past wars of this world and God shows me they are nothing like what He is up against with His own children. Fighting one another. Killing one another. The Spiritual Warfare that is killing God's children, killing their own creative nature and energy around them.

When I wake to the significance of this dream I am reminded of all the books I have written. The timelines within them. The messages and warnings within them. The Prophecy within them. I am reminded of all the things that have come true within them.

As I talk with Allison, (from the agency who wants to turn my books into a movie) yesterday it hits me that what I am doing is bigger than me. That what I have accomplished with my books and God's books is bigger than me. The project that was set in my lap is a huge mission handed to me from God; Himself. The Greatest and Wisest Being of this World and the Universe. He knows what He needs to sustain this world and His children. He has shown me what is going to happen if we do not wake up and turn this world around.

His warnings become very real to me this early hour of the morning.

I see the end of this timeline and come to realize; He has told me He has done it before, and He will do it again. That phrase is in reference to the 'Extinction' process I have seen coming. The one we as humans are creating on our own. By all the chemical and nuclear weapons. By all the dis-ease we keep reinventing and spreading. By all the hate we keep stirring up generation after generation.

This dream takes me way back to the desert when Jesus was tempted by the devil. When Jesus was shown the end of the world. This dream brings me back into *"Jesus Christ's Knowing"* the Father showed Him the end of the world, over 2,000 years ago!!!

(in this dream I see Saint Diana. The Princess of Wales. I see Prince Charles and I feel the end of her life, as a significance in this dream for some reason. She is being shown to me in this hotel for a reason).

History of the Waldorf Hotel: Waldorf Astoria New York

Later History: the first hotel, the 13-story, 450-room Waldorf Hotel, designed by Henry Janeway Hardenbergh in the German Renaissance style, was opened on March 13, 1893, at the corner of Fifth Avenue and 33rd Street, on the site where millionaire developer William Waldorf Astor had his mansion.

Number of rooms: 1,413

Number of restaurants: Peacock Alley, Bull and Bear Steakhouse, La Chine
Opened: 1931

Home to world leaders, royalty, movie stars, and music legends The Unofficial Palace

From its inception, the Waldorf Astoria was a true palace in the city Cultural figures, political leaders, musicians, and royalty gathered in its grand spaces and entertained in its opulent suites. The Waldorf Astoria's legendary service set the standards for American hospitality.

The Creation of a Legend

The original Waldorf Hotel was built at 33rd Street and Fifth Avenue in 1893 by William Waldorf Astor. Four years later, John Jacob Astor IV, William's cousin and familial rival, built an even taller hotel next door in an act of one upmanship. The cousin finally agreed to a truce and the two buildings were connected through a 300-foot marble corridor known as Peacock Alley. The Waldorf Astoria was born.

As I research this hotel, I find a photo of the man that looks like the man in the dream sitting up on his throne in the lobby of the hotel. The man who Jesus (or depicting Jesus) tells the owner of the hotel it stinks and has bad energy in it. William Waldorf Astor was dressed like the 'Wizard of Oz' sitting in the lobby of my dream.

1950-1963 Golden Age

From Fran Sinatra to Ella Fitzgerald, celebrities flocked to New York's unofficial palace. The Waldorf Astoria hosted legendary events like Prince Raimer III of Morocco and Grace Kelly's engagement party. President John F. Kennedy's birthday gala, the April in Paris Ball, and a special address by Queen Elizabeth II. The Duke and Duchess of Windsor made the Waldorf Astoria their home after the Duke abdicated the throne and the hotel welcomed every U.S. President from Herbert Hoover to Barack Obama.

Queen Elizabeth II spoke at the Waldorf Astoria in 1957...

(Princess Diana shows up in my dream for some reason)!!!

I research the Waldorf Astoria in New York City for that is what came up. In the dream I felt as if this hotel was in Las Vegas. The city of Sin.

The Hotel felt like dirty money. It felt like negative and extremely bad energy.

As I wake from the dream and research the history of the hotel, I am reminded of my adventure and grand stay in California. When I went all by myself to California and attended the Pitch Fest with Author house Publishing. I am reminded how I felt in those few short days. Living in the grand hotel which I cannot even remember the name of.

I remember it was off Merv Griffin Street. I remember being scared to death most of the time and I was in such a large city by myself trying to make it big with my story.

I ask the Lord to help me open doors with our books and I wonder if this is what He is showing me. The dirty money and the knowing I won't be able to handle all the money that it will bring in.

So, is God showing me He doesn't want me to move forward?

Is He showing me what hotel I may stay in some day once the books get made into a movie?

I never know the full picture until God has it unfold. I, however, do know He shows me a painful world if we do not wake up to reality and start helping the less fortunate than ourselves. If we do not start getting a handle on the healthcare issues and the mental health issues that are drowning His children in sorrows. God shows me 'we are in trouble'.

You've always had the Power my dear, you just had to learn it for yourself.
-Glinda-
Wizard of Oz

Bella Louise Allen

9:00 p.m.

February 14, 2021

I wake on the couch at work. It's cold all around me this morning. After yesterday's healing and teaching session with a 29-year old woman trying desperately to survive the *"Spiritual Emergence"* that she is experiencing, I have more Native American energy surround and present themselves this morning.

I see a man. He gives me his name; *"Blanket in the Sun"*. I am not sure which tribe he is from. I see his shining skin. His face glows. He is in full headdress this morning. I see the black and white feathers that run down the back of his shoulders. As He stands before me, I see his smile. He is proud of me for believing. He is proud of me for teaching the sacred heritage and rituals. He is proud of me for taking this child under my wings.

I have tears in my eyes as I speak the words, "I'm not trying to take anything away from your people's. I am trying to show them how powerful and beautiful your rituals, and your peoples are. I am trying to connect them back to the Light which they have come from.

Blanket in the Sun shares with me; *"I see you are on a peaceful mission, for all people's".*

"We will assist you in any way we can".

"Just ask and it will be given".

As I speak briefly with *"Blanket in the Sun"*, He smiles, and our hearts will be connected as one on this journey from this day forward.....

I had a dream in the night, yet I can't pull it forward. I feel the dream, yet I can't remember it.

That is my telltale sign, I am not supposed to remember it.

I lay and converse with the Lord. A lot has transpired in the past few days. All good things. So many good things I wonder what will unfold in the next few months. I feel as if everything I have worked for is going to come to fruition, yet my heart warns me, to go slow and breath as these new doors open.

I lay this morning in the dark after an amazing encounter with a special soul who shows himself to me. To help me understand I am well loved and respected for my belief in the Indian Heritages and cultures. As I lay and go over my communication and the death of Miss Felicia, I feel her in my arms as I lay on the couch. For the first time in a long time I hold this angel's spirit on my chest as I lay on the couch. No tears. No crying. Just the knowing God placed her in my arms in the fall of 2015 and I was accepting of all He showed me and all He asked of me.

I come to understand this morning of the power behind what may come from this love story coming to the public. I come to understand the healing that can occur for many.

I have been connected the past few days with, "Near Death Experience" sites on face book. Those searching and looking for answers and looking for a connection to their loved ones in spirit. As I am continually learning I am held up and pushed forward daily by the Spirit of God, I come to understand as I post and answer some of the questions brought forward, I am doing counseling and have been for months.

The book "Into the Fires of Hell", the second book I wrote in this series, was the book the Lord and I wrote together as He showed me what my future career would be. I have taken care of the elderly and dying for such a long time. I tell Him I would love to move forward into my new career soon. I would love to help others and ease their pain from the loss of their loved ones.

Yesterday in my session with my new client I felt such love from the Native American Culture and people's as I showed her how to center, clear and connect with her heritage. I gifted her with many things yesterday. Rites, rituals and traditions was just one of the many things I gave her. I brought in her 'higher-self'. I brought in her 'future-self'. I introduced her to 'Gwendolyn'. An angel I have met before but was not aware of who she was. A message she brought me; and these two angels come together. Past, present and future merging together. I come to understand more than I was ever expecting yesterday. We opened 'Akashic Records' for my client and myself. Generations of knowing unfold in our three-hour session yesterday. Lessons beyond me? No, they are lessons within me, waiting to be let out. Waiting to be passed on and learned from.

Many tribes we come from. Many tribes call out to us. If we are brave enough to listen. If we are brave enough to see the truth behind the "Great Spirit in the Sky". We can learn who we are as Spiritual Beings. We can learn who we are as Human Beings.

We listened to and brought in our Native American ancestors by listening and connecting with drumming music. Smudging and sending up our prayers for a deeper connection for my new client. We listened to a cd I used on my own Shamanic journey back in 2015 as I learned all Spirit are connected as one. No race, religion or creed outshines the other. We are all come from the Light.

I show my client what "Sacred Rituals" are and I open my story to a woman who can make a change in this world for herself, her son and those she comes into contact with. I open her heart to the love that waits for her from her higher-self. We opened her Akashic Records yesterday and I surprised myself by opening the portal for her, with the assistance of her own angel brigade. They now wait for her to connect through meditation and prayer. They now wait to see what lessons they may be able to teach her about her own lineage, her own soul-path and the purpose of why God created her. The reason God saved my life. Was to teach and pass on all the great knowledge He knew was inside me all along.

Song of the morning: *Take the ribbon from your hair...*

As I open my heart and let the Lord lead me daily, He sings this song to me this morning. I see the Creator opening doors and letting my hair down, relaxing and learning to trust in the Lord is something He wishes for me today. I hold Miss Felicia and her story in my heart and God reminds me; *"You will break their hearts with this love story".*

Help Me Make It Through the Night...

Take the ribbon from my hair
Shake it loose and let it fall
Lay it soft upon my skin
Like the shadows on the wall
Come and lay down by my side
Till the early morning light
All I'm takin' is your time
Help me make it through the night

Song by: *Sammi Smith*

The Lord shows me, I help Him bring Light back to this darkened world, by believing and trusting in His plans for me. I see the underlying message in this song, He brings it forward and sings to me. I have helped aid and assist many in those last moments of death. Days, hours and minutes before they transition from this cruel painful world into the next world. The Light. I help others return to the Light from which they have come from. This song comes forward to enlighten me of the many sleepless nights I have been there for God and His children. Comforting them in there darkest hours. He shows me again our special bond and connection through this love song.

Bella Louise Allen

6:30 p.m.

February 14, 2021

Spirit is overly active today. My head feels as if my crown is wide open and I feel them hug and squeeze me tight today. I feel the hands of God inside my consciousness today as He reminds me I AM.

I worked an overnight shift last night and my client; seems more tired and finds it frustrating for her mind is sharp and her body is weak. Her frustration for not being able to do the things she was hoping to do at the end of those sparing moments in her life. Her shoulder surgery did not work, and she wishes to go back to have it replaced, yet her health is not good to undergo another surgery.

I share with my client, a 93-year old client who is a widow, mother, grandmother and great- grandmother, my story. Pieces of who I am for she loves to hear the stories of Jesus and me walking together. I get to share with her the excitement of my phone call from Allison. The woman who stated she is going to be having all three of my books that are published reviewed for adaptation for a movie. I hold onto hope this weekend and the excitement builds and the project and plans the Lord has shown me for over ten years gets a little closer to reality.

Manifesting with Jesus Christ and so much love is felt today. The angels feel it, I feel it and the Lord sits back and smiles at me today.

It's Saint Valentine's Day today and I have no one to send me a romantic card to open and admire. I have no one to snuggle with tonight when I finally get to go home after two long shifts back to back. I get not flowers delivered to brighten my day. Yet, the Lord shows me He is opening doors for our love story. Something He is anxious to have come to light.

Today we open another book. A special book we write together. As I come to understand all my writings and my soul-purpose and my predestined incarnated life, I am asked to write and share more of my gifts. I find the Lord directs my face book page to metaphysical sites. I see He opens Near Death Experience Sites. He opens radio stations dealing with Psychic Interviews and Conversations. We seem to be practicing for our upcoming 'debut'.

Three days ago; I continue to feel and know of the energy of the movie stars, talented singers and comedians. God is opening the doors for what my reality truly is. I run with my angels. I sing with my angels and I play act with my angels. I feel more and more like Robin Williams. I feel as if the angels are literally coming to life within me. Some days I feel as if I will float off the floor. Today the 'arctic air' seems to be surrounding me. The wings of the angels and the atmosphere of the universe seems to be all around me. The Higher Realms and the Higher Angels Presence is what that reminds me of.

I was given the name "Dale Earnhardt".

I was given "Jerry".

I was given "Libby's" name.

I was given "Mission".

"Mission statement".

I was given "Top Gun". I keep play acting with 'Henry Fonda'.

I take a bath two days ago and 'Penny Marshall's' face is shown to me. I am shown "Ron Howard's" face and then "Little Opie".

I am reminded of the movies, sit-coms and the many movies I have seen the Lord play out on my spiritual eyes over the past eleven years. Only the past five plus years have I recorded these messages and visions. Painful knowing of what God's world has turned into. What God has shown me. God and the His Son, Jesus Christ asked me to record those messages and I did. As painful as it was, I did it out of my deep passionate love for them Both.

So many playful angels present around me today. Miss Felicia seems to be like a monkey on my back the past few days. Her presence has never left me. The

Lord just wouldn't allow me to see or feel her. I needed to finish this project, to get it right where it is today, I had to let that painful piece of this puzzle go.

As we get closer to what God's Plans are, I see on television tonight the reality again; that he is showing me. God is opening the doors.

I sit at work and we watch the Golden Girls. A most humorous sit-com and I absolutely love Estelle Getty. The mother of Bea Arthur.

Stage names, and play actress's and actors brought forward to help me over the years to fantasize and learn my signs and symbols.

This afternoon as I sit and watch this show, I see a bright illuminated white circle beside me. It was shone to me quickly, as all my visions are. The Lord tells; *"you're a quick study and I don't have to repeat myself too many times, for you are on spot most of the time".*

I see the white orb beside me. The same one I saw yesterday as I was giving a client of mine lessons on how to ground and protect herself and give her little messages that I received in yesterday, before she arrived.

My new client's future-self showed up. Hard to understand I work in the past, stay present in the moment and see the future of many things.

As I see and recognize the angel *"Gwendolyn"* who was brought to me maybe six months ago, I come to realize she is showing me a big kiss. I see the lips. Painted deep purple and with like a million stars on them. I see I am receiving a kiss for my client from yesterday and her mother, Judy.

Not 10 minutes goes by and I receive a text message wishing me a Happy Valentine's Day from the woman who was desperately seeking help for her daughter who is experiencing her own *"spiritual emergence'.* I feel heartwarming love as I come to realize the angels knew she was going to text me. The purple kiss was my *'warning'* or heads up. The white orb present let me know who was coming through or let me know someone close to her was coming through and then I receive the message, of Happy Valentines from Judy and her daughter's family.

As I tell Judy this, I tell her I am watching *"The Golden Girls"* and she tells me that's too funny.

That was my mother's favorite show. I tell her about the deep purple lips and the sparkling shiny stars on the lips and Judy tells me purple was her mother's favorite color.

Just a glimpse into my world as I sit and watch a special woman who lays in bed 24-7 waiting for the Lord to take her home.

My clients husband passed away a few years back. My client suffers with dementia. She has 5- second recall and she is very repetitive with her thought process. She calls me nurse and all the other women who care for her, she calls nurse.

Sometimes I like to test her, and she always aces this one little test. I am the only one that she can remember the name of. I ask her, to test her, I say; *"Rose, what's my name."* She waits, she thinks and then she smiles and says; *"your name is Bella".* Something so little brings a smile to my face.

Rose is a special soul and she is only one of a million or more that the Lord sees need taking care of. Only one issue in the healthcare crisis that He sees needs attention. Today as I care for Rose her son-in-law visits. Her daughter is home and has been sick for a while now. Rose is unaware of her daughter being sick. She wouldn't remember it if they told her.

Rose's son-in-law brings her supper from Olive Garden. He brings her a box of chocolates and a Valentines card. He brings her a tiny stuffed animal and out of all these gifts she goes wild and cries when she sees this tiny little stuffed dog. His fur is a golden yellow color. He looks like a little golden retriever. Rose is obsessed with the color gold. She has things throughout her home that are all gold. Trinkets and vases and mirrors and shiny boxes that are all lite up and it looks like a house of pure gold. (none of these things are gold, they just look like it). An amazing woman I take care of today. A blessing to be able to assist her in her last days before she goes home. Before she crosses over into the Light of God. Another sad story that breaks my heart as I sit with her and know her family pays nearly $20,000.00 a month for her care. Just for her care for one year is $240,000.00, that's an expensive way to live the last days of your life. Her household expenses and food expenses are not included in that hefty price. I have assisted her for over a year and she has had 24-7 care longer than that. An expensive painful knowing of what so many families are dealing with.

Rose's house may have things that look like there made of gold, but she by no means is rich. She used to be a bookkeeper. Not a very glamorous or famous job. She probably did alright in her day, but I'm sure her savings if she had any is probably gone by now.

Song of the day the angels bring it forward in the kitchen at work tonight. I wonder what the meaning or hidden message is? I feel it has a little something to do with waiting and being patient and enjoying life while you can. Before it's too late. Making each moment count, maybe?

I hear the undertone of God is opening doors and the books are ready to be seen and finally appreciated for the Love Jesus Christ has waiting for those who will see what He has done for me. Those He sees will '*Roll the stone away from His Tomb*'. The words He had me speak to Allisson three days ago.

Song of the Day: *Sitting on the Dock of the Bay*

> Sitting in the morning sun
> I'll be sittin' when the evening comes
> Watching the ships roll in
> Then I watch em' roll away again, yeah.
> I'm sittin' on the dock of the bay
> Watchin' the tide roll away, ooh
> I'm just sittin' on the dock of the bay
> Wastin' time

Sung by *Otis Redding*

History of Otis Redding: The History of Otis Reading is the first of numerous compilations of Otis Reading songs, featuring hits from 1962 to 1967. Released one month prior to his death in December 1967. It was the final album (and only compilation album) issued during his lifetime.

Album: History of Otis Redding Released: November 1967 Genre: Deep Soul Southern Soul Length: 31:35

Label: Volt

On its final approach to Madison on December 10, 1967, however, the private plane carrying soul-music legend Otis Redding would crash into the frigid waters of a small lake three miles short of the runway, killing seven of the eight men aboard, including Redding.

Message:

I am reminded of the songs from the Cranberries this week. *"Dolores"* the name comes forward and I find out after being nudged tonight, who this Dolores is.

Dolores O'Riordan's death, *"In the End and disbandment"* (2016-2019)

In October 2016, the Cranberries received a BMI Award in London for three million radio plays in the United States of their single *"Dreams"* taken from their debut studio album. The award had been presented with a special citation of achievement.

As I record today's messages and the past few weeks puzzle pieces start fitting together, I see so many underlying clues that prove God has been working toward something beautiful.

He is shining a huge light into this world, through this love story. I wonder if this project and mission of mine will produce the love that He shows me it could, if someone just picked up the books and read the Love He has for Humanity. To recognize the Love Our God has for His own children.

Messages coming in at the speed of light today. I hear song after song and then I play act with the angels. I hear the song from *"Smokey and the Bandit"*.

"He's found a dime, loaded up and truckin'." She's gonna do what they say can't be done"....

"Jerry's" name coming in for the past two days. I understand Jerry Reed sings this song and God fanaticizes and plays with me as we get closer to opening the doors to His Miracle.

3:05 a.m.

February 15, 2021

As I wake at the be-witching hour this morning, I see Saint Padre Pio watching me in my room. I wake with the sense and feel of his ghostly presence. His Spirit surrounding me as I sleep. This sweet soul has been with me on my journey since the beginning. I was not always aware of him though. More than a few times I have felt his powerful presence and I always asked, "why do I feel as if I will pass out when he shows up, in my life"?

I am reminded again of my soul purpose and my path. My own past life. My own soul-self. I am shown again by God, as I sleep; He shows me again as His sweet Mother Mary.

Another ritual done in the night as I sleep. Something I have done before. Something I feel I am drawn to by my Indian ancestors. Something I do this morning as I sleep to remind God knows the seeds of His children.

I am asked to share it all. To not hold back anything. I write freely and without shame or guilt. I write what I write for the Truth shall rise after today.

I vibrate in the chair as I write. I feel the back of my consciousness as if the *"mouth of God"* is wide open to my consciousness. Something that usually happens when I feel Our Father's Powerful Presence. Something I first felt strongly just before I go to meet with Father M. My creator steps forward and shows Himself to me. Through the very back of my head. Where my spinal column meets and connects to my skull.

My Lichen Sclerosis is itching and burning in the night. As I sleep and as I am vulnerable and open to all that is, I feel it get worse in the night. Something I experience most nights as I let myself go and relax. The burning of my very soul for my creator comes to life in the night. I have come to understand this dis-ease and manifestation from the eyes of God. I have come to understand it as a burning deep in the core of me. A burning in my very soul for the creator.

The doctors have struggled for over three years to treat it. The doctors have told me they don't know a lot about it yet.

I am told and shown by the Lord, that it is just as I have described. A burning from the very core of me. A burning off, from my root chakra. As I rest in the night and try my best to sleep, I feel the hands of God upon me. I feel Him surround me and I feel my body ache. As this occurs I lay my own hands on my triangle patch at my core. I feel the dry, flakey and itchy places on the skin on my outer vaginal wall. It burns deep into the layers of my flesh. The Father explains it is the generational abuses experienced within my family. Within the past lives of all those women connected in my lineage. Sexual abuses over the years experienced. Passed down and driven mad because of such horrific abuses to God's women. I come to understand something that is beyond me. I come to see; what may be something very real for more than just me. I am shown a dis-ease and ailment of my own. Something that has plagued me for three years. Something the doctors can't seem to find a treatment for.

My physical body seems to be in good shape, yet all the years of neglect keep it from being in good health. A struggle I have had for such a long time. My spirit is full of life. I feel young and vital, yet my physical body feels somedays as old as one hundred years old. The strain and knowing I haven't been able to take care of myself, because I have been taking care of so many others my entire life.

During the night as I sleep, not more than an hour ago, I lay my own hands over my core, my root chakra and I try to heal myself. I feel the Father's hands guide me. I do a sweeping motion and I pull at the hair on my patch. I do a motion as if I pick the very seed at my core out. I do a dropping motion as if to drop the seed that was inside of me on the floor.

As God reminds me in this restful state, while I am in between sleep and the awake state, of the knowledge of my past life of Eve. I am reminded of the fact He continually tells me I am Mary as well. I am shown again, and He gives me proof of it every day. The souls merging. The veils lifting. The Truths Rising. I am shown Mother Mary standing right in front of me. Her face is looking to the left. She looks to the past and she is standing right in front of me. Something to be revealed. Something to be shown. Something God is showing me as I sleep.

After the ritual in my sleep of dropping the seed on the floor, I see Saint Padre Pio walking around my bed. A special soul, who was very gifted and talented. A Catholic Mystic. A healer and theologian. A man who spent hours in prayer getting to know Jesus Christ and Our Father.

"The farther back you look the farther forward you can see". Quote by Winston Churchill.

A quote I used many years back in my writings. It resurfaces as I write about the truth I am shown in my dream state tonight.

Past lives lived is what God is unveiling to me as I hold His Hand and walk further into the Light He shines before me.

My Reiki Master Teacher, Kathy sends me a link for mediation last night. Something that happens in the moments just when I need it to move forward. A meditation on the *'vortex'* and sleeping. The VORTEX by Abraham Hicks. I breath in and out through the whole mediation just before I go to bed. I open to the truth of my existence. As I create with God the Truths of my life and soul path, I become more enlightened to who I am and why I have been incarnated in this lifetime. Shining light onto God our Creator this morning. An amazing experience as I wake seeing Saint Padre Pio walking around in my bedroom. He walks into my life and shows me he has seen all I have done in my life. He walks around just moments after I'm shown me; as Mother Mary waiting to be unveiled of the truths, God has given to me.

Bella Louise Allen

Message:

Love songs to connect me to the One who created me. Love songs to show me just how much God loves me. Adele has been a special musician I have connected back to my truths with. She has enlightened me to my truths of my existence. She has two special c.d.'s. 21- which is my birthdate and 25- which is Jesus Christ's birth date. Numbers do matter and I work in alchemy and know that God's heart is connected to my own. He is enlightening His love for me and all of mankind...

*

8:30 a.m.

Today at mass the Lord shows His playfulness the closer we get to wherever it is He is taking me. He sits with me. He stands with me and He kneels and prays with me at Saint Mary's this morning. I attend mass after my overnight shift last night. Today as I stand before His cross on the Altar He stands up with me and motions as if He hits a homerun. I feel His robe that he wears in most of my visions. Plain white and it has dust and dirt on it. He shows me He hits the bat with His left hand and the ball goes all the way to the outfield. He tells me; *"The bases are fully loaded, and we are going to make a grand slam, homerun with this project".*

Jesus Christ shows me this morning He is bringing this love story home for the children of this world.....

Bella Louise Allen

1:00 p.m.

February 17, 2021

The Lord brings me to new heights of His knowing today. The closer we arrive to Easter the more my own heart pains me. The death and torture of Our Dear Lord is something I have been living for the past five years. A painful knowing, I cannot erase out of my memory. I have been seated at the foot of Christ's cross and He reminds me I have viewed it firsthand before.

My reality is a painful knowing of the Great I AM and today at mass I see the love the Catholic Church holds by keeping the rites of Christ alive. The Holy Eucharist celebration shines a light on His Word and the Ashes today sprinkled on our heads is a sign of His sacrifice for all of Humanity. Today is Ash Wednesday and I receive this special rite with the Lord standing within me. Our Father shines His Light upon me daily now and He watches my every move. He feels my every breath go in and out of my body.

I bow my head in prayer this morning and I see a large black and red checkered cross. My eyes are closed, and I see a cross that is covered in blood and death. The red and black represent just that. I see there is an underlying theme with the red and black and it has to do with 'Paul" Bunyan. An icon for the state of Maine and the town of Bangor, Maine. A huge statue that stands at the Cross-Insurance Center. In the center of this checkered cross, I see the words, "WASHINGTON" in bold lettering. It goes straight down the center of this cross.

At the foot of the cross I see a red fern growing up out of the ground. I see this fern is healthy and in full bloom. Bright red leaves on this fern as it is snug to the ground beneath the cross. I associate a special movie from my childhood with the red fern. It portrayed a young man who raised a couple of coon dogs. He had a female and male dog he trained to hunt racoon. A young boy that grew up in the backwoods and he gave his whole heart to raising these special animals. "Ann and Dan", is what he called these four-legged friends of his. In the movie *"Where the Red Fern Grows"*, is a great book about the adventurous story where a young boy and his dream for his own red-bone hound hunting dogs. Set in the Ozark Mountains during the Great Depression, Billy Coleman works hard and saves his earnings for 2 years to achieve his dream of buying two coonhound pups. He develops a new trust in God as he faces overwhelming challenges in adventure and tragedy roaming the river bottoms of Cherokee country with Old Dan and Little Ann. The story follows the inseparable trio as they romp relentlessly through the Ozarks, trying to tree the elusive Ghost raccoon. Their efforts prove victorious as they win the coveted gold cup in the annual coon-hunt contest, capture wily ghost coons and bravely fight a mountain lion. Through these adventures Billy realizes the meaning of friendship, loyalty and more. In the end the two loyal red-bone hounds end up dying. Little Ann dies after Old Dan is attacked by a mountain lion. Little Ann dies of a broken heart and Billy buries them side by side. In the spring Billy visits the grave of his two four-legged friends and finds a miraculous red fern growing right up between the two best friends he ever had. A sign of true love, for one could not survive without the other.

Message:

I see and feel the underlying connection between God showing me the red checkered flag, and then a red fern growing up beneath the foot of the cross. The wording of *"Washington"*, I believe has to do with the political struggle that has gone on for far too long. A nation and a world in turmoil and we need to make some fast decisions to come out of this painful pandemic and the healthcare crisis that is crippling a nation and the world.

I feel the Lord's pain this morning as Easter approaches. Memories shared with me of the reality God; Our Father witnessed the day His Son was tortured and hung from the cross. Today we witness it all over again. I see it every time I turn on the news and see a bombing of a synagogue or a shooting that takes the lives of those who gather to worship the Lord.

I see the huge cross Our Father carries as He tries to get the attention of all those who could make a difference. I remind Him, *"Time matters, and the lives of all our children matter".* I beg Him *to* open a door. I promise Him I will give it all to Him. Every penny of it. I will do my best every day to make something great happen if He only lets a light shine on His broken heart. A heart I continue to carry within my own.

Messages coming in last night and today and I am pushed to call my publishing consultant. He is a special man who helped me through a very rough time in my writing career. A friendship was created and today I get more messages with the vision at mass and Jeff shares with me he has suffered with two strokes since our last conversation. The doctors prepare him for his last days and I cry copious amounts of tears after I get off the phone with him. My best friend in the world, beside Jesus and I find out he won't be here with us much longer. I ask the Lord; "How much more can my heart take"?

"How many more will you let me lose before you take me home"?

God understands my heart and how many times it's been broken. I breath through the pain today and I release my best friend and his end walk in this world, to God. I can't help him. I can't do anything but reach out and talk and support him in the last days he has left.

I talk to Jeff about setting up some distance Reiki Healing time with him. I ask him to allow me to assist in the only way I know how. Visually sending love and through the atmosphere sending up the intention for the Lord to make a miracle happen. He has just purchased a book on energy healing, and I told Jeff that is the Lord nudging him. A powerful healing modality and when I went to visit him a few years back and met Jeff. He was scared and intimated by my powerful friendship and love for him. He wouldn't allow me to get to close to him and his mother has explained many things about her kindhearted loving son. His mother Jane is in the spirit world. I met Jeff's grandmother, mom, dad and grandfather before I reached out to him to publish my books. Messages coming in and names clicking after Jeff and I converse back in 2015, when I put my first book to print with his help. The angels setting up a love story like no other.

Messages coming in today as just before I receive the call back from him a gentleman in a security guard uniform walks beside me into Walmart. Jeff was a '*bouncer*' at a local bar in his hometown. I feel the energy of his dad and grandfather as I know the angels showing me the messages in the physical world. That's how close they are to me. Putting big bold messages in front of me, to make sure I don't miss them in the light of day. In the night-time in the dark, I see the film roll constantly in front of my eyes. Messages, angels and spirit reaching out to me to show me they're surrounding me.

Today I ask the Lord to hold Jeff tight. I want him to witness our movie. The project that God set in my lap I would love for him and my mom both to see this in the movies before they transition into the next world. I ask God today to speed up the process for it surely would be a wonderful gift to them both to see such a heart-warming love story revealed. Love, faith and hope for the world, and I wouldn't want to miss their tears or their smile for knowing my hard work and the Lord's hard work didn't go to waste. Messages of love from the creator and Jesus Christ in such dark times. What a better gift then to see the Second Coming of Christ come to light....

3:00 a.m.

February 20, 2021

In bed for a short while tonight. My heart feels restless and the closer we get to revealing our love story the more I start to feel the energy and the tears of sorrow I have cried for such a long time. I feel the pain of my whole life tonight. We get ready to shed light on my personal life and we expose all my truths.

My heart feels the sadness and knowing of what may or may not be taken in by others. I always fear judgment from those who don't fully understand where my heart lays. My heart has sought for love all my life and I lay alone again tonight in bed. I feel as if Christ steps back the past few days, so I can get some work done. I dislike that very much. We still talk on and off, yet I can't feel His powerful presence the past few days.

My head reels with excitement for what is to come. My body still vibrates like it has for over three years since I accepted His Holy Presence inside of me. His hands and His kisses he has pulled back from me tonight.

Today Christ allowed me to know of *"Lacey's"* presence around me. I knew right away when he said her name, who it was he was showing me.

Lacey Peterson is a woman who was murdered by her husband. Another horrific ending to an incredibly beautiful story. I see her name and then I see one delicate hand trying to reach out to me from the veil. It looks as if it is a photo from an ultrasound. I see the amniotic fluid sack that separates Lacey from this world. I come to understand she is reaching out to her family. A message and a knowing that she is happy. She and her baby. I don't get to see her baby. Yet, the way she was presented I come to understand immediately who God was presenting to me. The name Lacey and the hand that looked as if it was in the womb of a woman.

So many sad stories and the Lord promises the closer we walk to where He is leading me; He promises I will receive proper counseling. Something I truly feel I have not yet received. My broken heart torn out of my chest daily as so, many deaths revealed and so much tragedy in this world was revealed to me by Jesus Christ. A story I couldn't and didn't have time to make up.

I try to put some semblance of a cast of characters list together today. I try to focus it on the first three books and not the whole brigade of angels that have been working with me. I write up a list of songs to go with certain scenes in the movies. Special songs the Lord and I have been listening to repeatedly over the past five plus years as I learn what God's desires truly are.

As I wake this morning He reminds me of the Holistic Health and Healing Center. The bigger one that He wants raised once I start to receive some of the royalties from His movies, documentaries and finally a few dollars in from our books. Jesus shows me this is the sure path to what He needs to unfold.

Miss Felicia's presence is very real the past few days and even the past two weeks. To understand she breaks my heart as we continue to be patient to connect her story to her mother. I fear she may not understand what God's plan is. I don't want to hurt anyone. I want love for this sweet child to be portrayed and nothing more. I want her mother to know, God will never forget her pain or the painful end to her sweet little angel's life.

Jesus goes over those last moments of Miss Felicia's life with me the past few days and it is so hard to remember all those painful truths. To know He continues to show me her own dad killed his own little girl out of fear of not getting or having what he needed in this life. Money truly is the root of all evil. Drugs have taken over the very lives of God's children. I see and know of His needs and as we get closer to opening this case wide open, I hope for a miracle and maybe some healing for Miss Felicia's mother and her brothers. May this project shine a light back onto their family and may they know God holds her in His arms and she is very loved by so many in heaven.

A love story to break the world's heart is what I believe God has me write for Him. So many loses and they spread out like the weaving of a giant spider's web. Something God has shown me. The many sad stories that are connected to my own. The very reason I lost my heart and my own mind. Painful times in my life shared with the world.

I prepare for my Reiki client in the morning. My friend Betty is coming to release some pain and tears from her own heart. I will hold that space so she can feel some relief. Her grandchildren have shut her out of their life and her son doesn't contact her for years and Betty just wonders why after all these years they can't have a family life together. They won't answer her text messages or phone calls and her heart was broken yesterday when her granddaughter never responded to her birthday wishes to her. Sad reality as the family structures continue to fall apart.

I worked on putting the presentation together for my lecture on the importance of writing and journaling daily for those with mental illness and drug addiction. I will be attending my first lecture on the importance of journaling and writing your story. I know God is preparing me for the next steps on my journey. It's sure to be amazing for it is God's plan. To shine His light in the world again. To bring His Love back down to earth. May all your wishes come true my Lord, and may this love story reveal the true You, that so many have forgotten.

Bella Louise Allen

7:31 a.m.

February 20, 2021

Another beautiful morning and I wake up with Saint Diana waking me. She stands at my bedside. One of many in my angel brigade. I hear the angels singing, *"only the lonely"* by Roy Orbison. A hidden message in the name of the song and the singers name.

I wonder what today will bring. As I am shown so many beautiful things now. Diana Princess of Wales has been with me for such a long time. I haven't always felt her or known she was there for there are so many angels around me. This morning she reminds me; "I was lonelier with Charles in my life, than without him".

"Your such a brave woman and one I admire you for all your strength".

"This child, Miss Felicia that you never once forgot loves you like a real grandmother".

"You shouldn't worry so much about what might be a negative outcome, but the beauty your creating".

"You have brought to life the heaven that everyone dreams about".

Saint Diana (as God calls her), has become a special friend that I could have never dreamt up. To see our hearts are so similar and playful. God knows her and I both through and through. Our children are our world. From the beginning to the end of it all. The title in the song, *"Only the lonely"* is brought forward for I really wish I could talk with someone in the physical world about how painful it has been to experience this sweet child's death over and over again. Diana also knows as do the rest of the angels all the rest of this story. The sad heart-breaking truths Jesus and the angels have shown me. All the deaths and events that I was shown before they happened. Blood pouring out a young girl that was in representation of Mr. Trump's daughter in connection to *'the Ariana Grande concert and shootings'.*

President Obama and Martha Washington sitting to the left of me, (which represented the past) as we looked on from the balcony. I felt the energy of the old south, in this dream). A young girl in the streets standing alone and she wears her confirmation dress and white gloves, in representation of *"JFK's assassination".* I didn't see it coming when the bullet struck her chest and blood poured down the front of her pure white dress before her body fell to the street. I woke up in tears and such surprise. An arrow pierced my heart for days after that dream and knowing was brought to me. Then the shootings occurred. The knowing that Christ revealed to me. "The Arianna Grande Shooting". A horrific story unfolded that day and God allowed me to see it before it happened. All writing in the books, not yet revealed.

'The Parkland shootings' was one of many more sad stories brought to me, by the Lord.

Mother Mary steps forward within my body. Mother Mary was showing the anger behind the young boy who committed that terrible massacre of innocent children and teachers. The name *"Connor"* brought to me on the winds. Mother Mary repeats for five minutes while I wail in bed, "Dead sparrows falling everywhere", "Dead sparrows falling everywhere". Repeatedly she spoke those words through my heart. Then I hear of the shootings at Parkland School. A terrible reality I have held under my heart and hat while I write, work and try to get the Catholic Church to counsel and direct me with the Lord's books.

The Lord even showed me Robin Williams last moments and in a way I could understand his state of fear and emotion behind his last acts before he hung himself. Robin was in a wicker chair which represented the many facets of his beautiful mind and the heavy cross he carried in those last days before he hung himself. Not an easy decision to make and it tortures the soul and I am familiar with that painful struggle of the dark night of the soul. I lived it since I was a teenager.

Jesus reminds me no one else was meant to write about His Second Coming but me. Diana reminds me this morning *"Focus on the end results of your efforts for your going to break millions of people's hearts."*

"They will come out of the woodwork to help you, now".

"The storm of the century and the story of the century, colliding together to bring back the Light of God".

"What a legacy to leave your own children". "You amaze me and take my breath away".

A brief encounter this morning as I wake after a restless night. I feel the power of God vibrating me all night long. I can't feel His Presence as much when I work and focus on getting our project to the finish line. The black and red checkered flag on the cross was part of this story coming in for the win. The last lap and leg of the race for me.

"So, close yet so far" A message early on in our communication. I can only hope for something beautiful this morning to come soon, for my spirit and body are exhausted.

2:03 a.m.

February 21, 2021

I wake on the couch at work. Hard to imagine I see so many beautiful things while I sleep. This morning Whitney Houston presents herself as a little black cherub. I see her beautiful smile. She has the purest white wings against her beautiful black skin. I see the colorful dress she has, and it fits her spirit perfectly. She reminds me of tinker bell in the movie *"Hook"*. I see her smile from one end of her face to the other. She brings me the knowledge that she sees what I am doing. Her presence in my life is not only through music when I listen to her on my c.d.'s it is all the time. Watching in the wings as I write and push forward every day to get Jesus Christ's project to the public. She brings me her knowing and her love for my pushing forward bravely every day.

Whitney tells me how heartbreaking it has been to see it from my eyes as God shares the angels He has graced me with. That they know my broken heart and my many tears for so many in connection to my broken heart.

As I wake from this dream, I see Whitney is showing me her own inner child has been awakened and she flits and flutters around this morning in my consciousness and shares with me, she supports and loves me for staying strong through it all. Especially when I was scammed 2 times and my hopes of Oprah helping with this Holistic Health and Healing Center all went south.

Whitney tells me; "Don't ever give up girl". "You got this and your gonna knock their socks off"!!

Whitney reminds me to keep my spirits elevated for they all love my music selections. It raises their spirits as my own soars with them. No matter where I am, they are there too.

My second appearance from the angels this morning after a lengthy session of putting the finishing touches on my visual presentation for the production company *"Bright Lights"*. I push myself as usual to finish before the deadline, I feel I am running against. To get God's word out is my main goal.

God brings Miss Felicia back to me and she twirls and flits and dances all around me this morning. Her spirits are high, and she can't wait to have her mother witness all the love God has put into getting her story to be seen. A center in memory of this sweet angel so those who need Jesus in their lives can reap the rewards of natural healing and Christ's word, always and forever will be heard around the world. No matter how dark it seems, His Light will always shine brighter than the darkness.

Robin Williams steps forward as I sleep. I see a large line of his family members standing behind him. An ongoing joke when Robin gets my mouth in trouble, I tell Robin; *"Go home your mother wants you"*.

So many heartwarming jokes this special angel has brought forward. I could never record them all for I am either driving or working and it comes in like a rain fall of words and gestures through my body. He tells me; *"no one understood the reality I was living any more than you do."*

Robin shows me his face up close this morning and I see his mouth is in a scrunched-up gesture. His shoulders pulled up close to his ears in a tortured stance. He has tears in his eyes as he shows me he knows the writings I have tried so hard to get someone to notice. The pleas of Gods, written for over five years and Robin Williams has seen them.

He shows me a needle this morning and says; "You're so sweet." "I'd inject a thousand needles of your kind of love straight into my veins if I could experience your kind of love".

He tells me; "Never give up on your dreams, for that is what life is made of". "What Dreams May Come"; is you and your sister's story, as you come through the horrible knowing and awakening" "Just like the movie, I portrayed". "Such torture for so many with mental illness".

*

12:00 a.m.

I woke to the song by David Bowie, *"Put on your red shoes and dance the blues away"*. I hear this song repeated until I get up and write what the Lord was bringing forward. The reality I have been living with since the fall in 2015. I feel a colorful dream unfolding as I hear this song being played in my head while God vibrates inside my brain as I sleep.

My near-death experience or "True Death Experience", in March of 2012, led to many vivid dreams. The dreams I started to record in 2014 and then 2015 as I learned more and more of who I am and my soul path. These dreams have gotten brighter and have had more meaning to them.

As I wake to the song by David Bowie, *"Put on your red shoes and dance the blues away"*, I am reminded of *'The Wizard of the Oz"* and the dream the Lord keeps bringing forward. In my daytime. He will remind me of things repeatedly until I record it.

Doris, Jane and Hiram and Don my publishing consultants grandmother, mother, grandfather and father in spirit have been present around me since before I reached out to Scott. A special man, who supported me on this writing journey while I was receiving so much dark information to record for the Lord.

David Bowie singing this song brings in the knowing of theirs. Scott's family, throughout our communication, Jane, Doris and Hiram and Don always and forever show up and talk to me on *"Broadway"* in Bangor, Maine.

I always and forever felt the energy behind, *"Broadway musical"* or *"Broadway plays"*. As David Bowie presents this song to me I see a line of dancers in my dream. I see and feel the Wizard of Oz again while I am sleeping. I feel God; Our Father and He is playing with my consciousness again, as I sleep. I feel Him vibrating deep within my brain. It is hard to ignore Him when I feel Him so close.

At 11:11 p.m. I woke briefly to check my cellphone. I have been conversing back and forth and answering questions with a group on rocks, stones and gems. The properties and which ones are good in which areas of your life. In this post I made the mistake of telling this one woman who asked; *"What do you do to ward of real dark nightmare dreams"*?

I responded; *"There is no stone that can ward off your bad dreams, only Jesus Christ can do that"*.

Well, for the next several posts back and forth I was bombarded with hateful and snide remarks that broke my tender heart. Again, the Lord bringing forward my truth. I innocently try to remind people that without His strength within us the world can be a dark place. As this post and the people, *'women'* who are supposed to be of Love and Light attack me and my belief in Jesus Christ. I eventually have one woman ask me to explain my reasoning behind my strong statement of *"Jesus is the only rock I need in my life to ward off bad dreams"*.

Finally, after my tender heart was broken, the Lord works with me, through these emotions and my broken heart. He reminds me again with this post and conversing back and forth of what He is up against in this world. Many hardened hearted people harbor and feel such anger toward Him. His very name angers people. This lesson broke my heart and the Lord knows it.

My dream with David Bowie helps to lighten my reality. We have been witnessing to many things together since my full awakening. David Bowie showed up in my life and I was enlightened to the Ghost from Christmas past. I, in the night am brought that very Ghost. Jesus Christ and God the Father are the Ghost from Christmas Past. Enlightening me of a better world, as I dream. Colorful dreams and the Wizard of Oz brings forward the energy of Judy Garland and the yellow brick road. Following the Son is like that for me. Dark in so many parts of my life yet I keep following the light He illuminates at my feet and He tells me we will be great in the movies.

Fun and fantasy and no one can make your dreams come true quicker than Jesus Christ.

So, I listen to the song, *"Put on your red shoes and dance the blues away,"* sung by David Bowie, for there surely is a message in it for me because God brought it forward this morning at 12 a.m. He vibrated me awake until I recorded it for Him.

The books I write for the Lord continue. This book I will wrap up before Easter. The season of Lent is so special to Our Heavenly Father. A resurrection story written for Jesus Christ and the Lord and I work on putting the second *'Book of Dreams'* into print. Editing and compiling more communication with Jesus Christ, Abba; Our Heavenly Father and all the angels present and surrounding me. A special project to help raise money for a Holistic Healing Center in memory of all the *'little children'* who have lost their voice. Brought into a painful world and taken from this world, to the safe arms of the Father and His Son, Jesus Christ.

Remembering a few little angels and I hold them near to my heart.

Ayla Bell Reynolds, Tavielle Kigas, Angela Palmer, and Marissa Kennedy are just a few special souls from Maine who have touched the very heart and soul of God....

May you rest in peace in the heavens above!!

Glossary

Spiritual Emergence- *Spiritual crisis is a form of identity crisis where an individual experiences drastic changes to their meaning system typically because of spontaneous spiritual experiences. A spiritual crisis may cause significant disruption in a psychological, social, and occupational functioning.*

Plethora- *A large or excessive amount of (something).*

Qi- *The circulating life force whose existence and properties are the basis of much Chinese philosophy and medicine.*

Universal Law- *In law and ethics, universal law or universal principal refers as concepts of legal legitimacy actions, whereby those principles and rules for governing human beings, conduct which are most universal in their acceptability, their applicability, translation, and philosophical basis, are therefore considered to be most legitimate.*

Law of Love- *The liberating law of love can be summarized in: "Jesus"; said: "You shall love the Lord your God with all your heart, with all your soul, with all your mind, and will all your strength." This is the first commandment. And the second, like it, is this: "You shall love your neighbor as yourself".*

There is no other commandment greater than these. Mark 12:30-31

It is the fruit of the spirit which is love....

Bibliography

All works used here within:

Personal Experiences revealed most lessons within these writings.

Google websites:

Facebook: Proof of Life After Death- Mentoring Through Social Media

Facebook: Your Soul Guides You- Mentoring Through Social Media

Facebook: Healing Crystals-Know Your Crystals- Mentoring Through Social Media

U-Tube: Information on 'Spiritual Emergence"

History facts: Wikipedia sites used for most historical facts

Ending Note
From The Author

I want to thank all those who have taken the time to read and absorb 'Book of Dreams'. I have written over thirty- three books in this series. My writing career began in the year 2015 and It all started with my passion to share and heal from my own traumas. A sad story written as I try to understand all that I have survived. Miracles Among Chaos is the first book in a long series of books as Jesus Christ called out my name, to hold Him, and to love Him. My saving grace was the Lord. That one book led to two additional books put to print, "Love Letters in the Sand-Ayla's Faith" and then after eighteen additional books I braved the world of publishing again with "The Tree of Knowledge is Mary's Sweet Vine". Powerful books written with an overall theme of God lives on through us.

I hope nothing more than to share how we all can be survivors and it starts with self-knowledge and self-love. If we can't love ourselves then we won't have enough left inside of us to give to others.

May God bless you and keep you safe in His arms. May you too stand tall and be the hero your children are looking for. Put on your red cape and let your truths shine out from all that tries to hold you back. Break the chains, break the cycles and let's continue to teach our children they are so very loved. Let's teach our children to be their "own hero"...

Bella Louise Allen

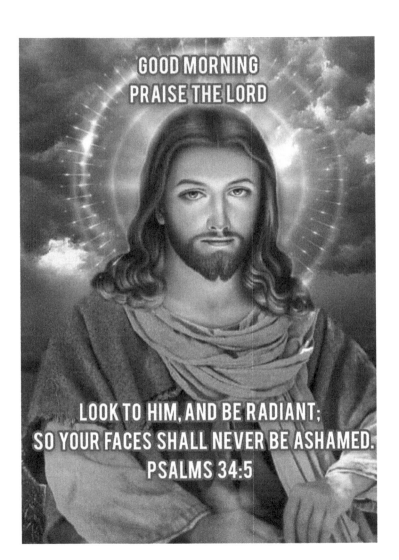

About the Author

Bella Louise Allen is an inspiring woman who has over come many obstacles in her own life. She shares the knowledge she has acquired over the years working with end of life care patients. Her own near-death experience has assisted her with the knowledge she shares in her writings. Her love for family is evident in all the books she has written. The love she portrays for the Lord shines bright and she gives a new perspective to the 'real Jesus', which many truly have not understood. Bella Louise shows the reader in her writings what a gift it is to care for others. She shows true passion and love for all those in her life that she cares for over her thirty-four years working with the elderly and dying. She is an inspiration to anyone who is looking for the light to shine in their lives. Her outlook on life inspires others to never let anything hold you back. She has a message of 'Being your own hero", is the only way to go today, in such a world full of negativity.

Printed in the United States
by Baker & Taylor Publisher Services

Printed in the United States
by Baker & Taylor Publisher Services